Herbert Puchta · Jeff Stranks · Peter Lewis-Jones

GRAMMAR PRACTICE

A complete grammar workout for teen students

HELBLING LANGUAGES
www.helblinglanguages.com

GRAMMAR PRACTICE 2
by Herbert Puchta, Jeff Stranks, Peter Lewis-Jones
© Helbling Languages 2012

The publisher would like to thank the following for their kind permission to reproduce the following photographs: **Dreamstime** p48 (women), p49 (Spain winning the World Cup in 2010); **©iStockphoto.com** p17; **NASA/ Bill Ingalls** p49 (Queen Elisabeth II); **Shutterstock** p48, p49, p62, p65.

ISBN 978-1-107-67761-6

Illustrated by Roberto Battestini, Giovanni Giorgi Pierfranceschi, Lorenzo Sabbatini, Nicola Zanni.
Printed by Athesia

All rights reserved; no part of this publication may be reproduced, stored in a retrieval system, or transmitted in any form or by any means, electronic, mechanical, photocopying, recording, or otherwise, without the prior written permission of the Publishers.

Contents

Introduction	04
Present simple – revision	05
Present simple and Present continuous – revision	08
Past simple – revision	10
Past simple – negation	12
Past simple – questions	13
Past simple – negation and questions	14
Past time expressions	15
Comparatives	16
Superlatives	18
as ... as	20
why / because	21
Directions (prepositions of place)	22
going to (revision)	24
going to – negative	25
might (not)	26
Present continuous for future	28
will – future	30
can for permission	32
should / shouldn't	34
have to / don't have to	36
must / mustn't	38
Shall we ... ? / How / What about ... ?	40
I'd prefer to ... / I'd rather ...	41
one – ones	42
Countable and uncountable nouns	43
some / any	44
Quantities	46
Irregular plurals	48
Questions with *who*	49
Adverbs of manner	50
whose + possessive *'s*	55
Possessive pronouns	56
Past participles	58
Present perfect	59
Present perfect + *already / yet*	62
Present perfect + *ever / never*	67
So (do/have) I / Neither (do/have) I	69
Appendix	71

Introduction

Dear student,

As you know, all serious sportspeople train regularly. Regular training means better performances in all sports from swimming to running, and football to table tennis. And soon what seems like hard work miraculously becomes more and more fun!

And grammar is no different. If you train regularly you make fewer mistakes, get better results and have much more fun. The exercises in both this book and the CD-ROM have been created so that they guarantee excellent results when done consistently. Ideally you should be practising your grammar in short frequent sessions rather than last-minute intensive bouts of study before an exam or class test. How about practising for ten minutes every day? Try it out and you'll soon see positive results!

You'll get the following support in both the book and the CD-ROM:

- the Contents list allows you to easily find the topics you want to practise
- each chapter starts with a summary of the most important topics and rules
- next to the summary there is a message from Professor Grammar, your mascot throughout the book. When you see the symbol, you can go to the CD-ROM.
- in the *How it works* section on the CD-ROM, Professor Grammar will explain specific grammar structures. Then go to the *Check it out* section to double-check you have understood everything.
- at this point you can decide whether you prefer to 'train' using the CD-ROM or the book. In the CD-ROM there are two or three exercises per chapter. Once you've done each exercise you can check your results by listening to the answer (LISTEN). But remember: listening to it first will not help you!
- in the book there are one or more pages of exercises per chapter. The exercises are ordered progressively according to difficulty, from the easiest to the most challenging.
- in the Appendix there is a list of all the grammar points, with tables and rules. Plus the answer keys.
- last but not least, each chapter in the CD-ROM has a cartoon with a fun quiz. Yes, Professor Grammar has some tricks up his sleeve to make sure you have fun while you are learning!

And now, what are you waiting for … let's get started!

All the best from the team of authors,

Herbert Puchta
Jeff Stranks
Peter Lewis-Jones

Present simple – revision

Hello! See me on the CD-ROM to discover more about the *present simple – revision* and to learn better when to use it.

You use the *present simple* when you want to talk about what someone always does, something that always happens or what someone feels. In negative statements and questions, you add **do / does** or **don't / doesn't**.

Where **do** you live?   I live in Birmingham.   I **don't** live in London.
Where **does** she live?   She lives in Manchester.   She **doesn't** live in Leeds.

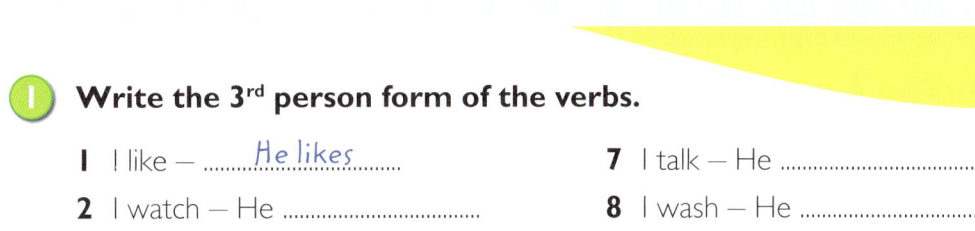

1 Write the 3rd person form of the verbs.

1 I like – He likes
2 I watch – He ....
3 I play – He ....
4 I am – He ....
5 I eat – He ....
6 I go – He ....
7 I talk – He ....
8 I wash – He ....
9 I leave – He ....
10 I buy – He ....
11 I switch – He ....
12 I have – He ....

2 Complete the sentences with the negative form of the verb and a word from the box.

football
novels
French
ham
~~red~~
the news
hip-hop
her sister

1 I wear black but I don't wear red .
2 Jack watches sports shows but he ....
3 Linda plays volleyball but she ....
4 Ian and Sophie study German but they ....
5 My parents listen to rock but they ....
6 You eat bacon but you ....
7 I like Mary but I ....
8 Trevor reads magazines but he ....

3 Rewrite the sentences and make them negative.

1 I like spaghetti
   I don't like spaghetti.
2 He lives in London.
   ....
3 You know Peter.
   ....
4 They play volleyball every Sunday.
   ....
5 Liam likes Jessica.
   ....
6 She wants to be a pilot.
   ....
7 Jenny and Rob are teachers.
   ....
8 We run 5 km every day.
   ....

4 Complete the text with the present simple form of the verbs.

Hi, my name ¹...is... (be) Oliver and my best friend ².............. (be) Paul. My best friend and I ³.............. (be) completely different. For example, he ⁴.............. (like) Geography and History, I ⁵.............. (like) Art and Music. He ⁶.............. (want) to be an archaeologist when he ⁷.............. (leave) school. I ⁸.............. (want) to be a film director. He really ⁹.............. (enjoy) all sports. I ¹⁰.............. (not like) sport at all. I ¹¹.............. (spend) all of my money on music. Guess what? He ¹².............. (not listen) to music. He always ¹³.............. (wear) black. I ¹⁴.............. (not like) black. My favourite colour ¹⁵.............. (be) blue. He ¹⁶.............. (hate) blue of course. I think there ¹⁷.............. (be) only two things we have in common: our age – we ¹⁸.............. (be) both 14 – and we both ¹⁹.............. (like) the same girl, Betty Hands. Betty ²⁰.............. (be) his girlfriend but I ²¹.............. (like) her too. Paul ²².............. (not know) this. I ²³.............. (not be) sure we are going to be best friends for much longer.

5 Use the text to write the questions for the answers.

1 What's Oliver's best friend called?
He's called Paul.

2 ....?
His favourite subjects are Geography and History.

3 ....?
He wants to be a film director.

4 ....?
No, he doesn't. He hates sport.

5 ....?
He buys a lot of music.

6 ....?
Blue.

7 ....?
They are both 14.

8 ....?
No, he doesn't know anything.

6 Write answers to the questions for you and your best friend.

	me
1 How old are you?	I'm ....
2 What are your favourite school subjects?	....
3 What kind of clothes do you usually wear?	....
4 What sports do you enjoy doing?	....
5 What do you usually spend your money on?	....
6 What job do you want to do when you're older?	....
7 What music do you listen to?	....
8 What do you usually do on a Saturday?	....

7 Write a short text about you and your friend. Use the information in 6 to help you.

My best friend is called ……………… . We're both ……………… . His favourite school subject is ………………
but my favourite is ……………… .

……

8 Use the pictures to complete the table.

On Mondays I		play tennis	but I don't go swimming.
On Tuesdays I			
On Wednesdays I			
On Thursdays I			
On Fridays I			
On Saturdays I			
On Sundays I			

And now go to the CD-ROM and do the *Cartoon for Fun!*

Present simple and Present continuous – revision

Do you remember? We use the *present simple* for habitual actions. We also use it for facts that are always true, and for feelings or thoughts. We use the *present continuous* for actions happening right now or in this period of time.

Present simple	Present continuous
I go to school every morning.	Today is Sunday, I'm staying at home.
The sun sets in the West.	We're studying the Romans this year.
I feel great today.	

1 Read the text and put the sentences in the correct column.

Paul and Jane live in a lovely cottage in the country. Paul travels all over the world for his job. Jane looks after the children. But they are staying in London at the moment. Today they are taking the children to the Natural History Museum. The children like dinosaurs and fossils. They are asking a lot of questions about them. And now they are inspecting a dinosaur's skeleton.

Present simple	Present continuous
....	....
....	....
....	....
....	....

2 Match the questions and short answers.

1 Does she usually drink coffee?
2 Is it raining?
3 Are you having lunch?
4 Do they speak French?
5 Do you think this is true?
6 Are you thinking about the match?

a No, I'm not.
b Yes, I do.
c No, they don't.
d Yes, I am.
e No, it isn't.
f Yes, she does.

3 Right or wrong? Correct the mistakes.

1 He's not understanding this rule.
....

2 Do you like watching TV?
....

3 Tom, why do you cry?
....

4 We are never eating meat.
....

5 Stop them. They are running away.
....

6 I don't do my homework today.
....

4 Write sentences with the present simple and present continuous. Use the verbs in brackets.

1 (go) I ....*go*........ on holiday to France every year. This year ....*I'm going*........ to Spain.

5 (have) In the morning, Andy usually .... But today he ....

2 (go) My dad usually .... to London by plane. Today .... by train.

6 (fall / not ride) Sandra sometimes .... off her bike. Today she .... her bike.

3 (meet) On Saturday afternoon, Monica usually .... Today she ....

7 (study / meet) In the evenings, James usually .... Tonight he ....

4 (play) Every Friday, Sam and Ben .... This Friday ....

8 (go / watch) On Sunday, we usually .... This Sunday we ....

Past simple – revision

Hello! See me on the CD-ROM to discover more about the *past simple – revision* and to learn better when to use it.

When you want to talk about things that happened in the past, you use the *past simple*. There are regular and irregular forms.

Regular	Irregular
play – play**ed**	go – **went**
talk – talk**ed**	read – **read**

I lik**ed** the present.

We **went** to the beach yesterday.

1 Tick the sentences that have got an irregular past tense in them.

1. She ran down the road and fell over. ✓
2. She phoned me and invited me to her party. ☐
3. We walked on the beach and played volleyball. ☐
4. He looked out of the window and saw me. ☐
5. She held his hand and kissed him. ☐
6. He climbed up the tree and jumped down again. ☐
7. We played tennis and then we went home. ☐
8. He read his book for five minutes and then he turned out the lights. ☐

2 Find the past forms. Write them beside the verbs.

1. go – *went*
2. break – ....
3. find – ....
4. give – ....
5. get – ....
6. have – ....
7. catch – ....
8. say – ....
9. read – ....
10. take – ....

H	B	R	O	K	E	S	N	T
A	R	G	E	T	W	E	N	T
F	O	G	O	T	O	C	A	G
O	K	R	P	O	G	A	V	A
U	E	E	E	O	L	U	E	V
N	D	A	A	K	P	G	R	E
D	C	D	R	E	A	H	E	V
W	O	H	A	D	E	T	D	E
E	N	T	H	A	S	A	I	D

3 Use the verbs from **2** to complete the sentences.

1. Yesterday I *went* into town.
2. I didn't watch TV last night – I .... a book!
3. My mother .... something to me, but I didn't hear her.
4. For Christmas last year, I .... a new bicycle from my parents.
5. I was dirty from playing football, so when I got home I .... a bath.
6. I was lucky yesterday – I .... a £20 note in the street.
7. My brother went fishing yesterday – he .... six fish!
8. We went on holiday to Greece last year – I .... hundreds of photos!
9. Last Friday, the teacher .... us lots of homework for the weekend.
10. Mary was angry with me because I .... her new MP3-player.

4 Complete the text with the past forms of the verbs in the box.

eat
give
~~wake up~~
go
dream
watch
meet
walk

1 Yesterday was perfect. I ...**woke up**... late.
2 I .... bacon and eggs for breakfast.
3 I .... DVDs all morning.
4 After lunch I .... roller-skating with my friends in the park.
5 I also .... Kevin Maley in the park.
6 He .... me a rose.
7 Then he .... home with me.
8 I .... about Kevin all night.
I can't wait until tomorrow!

5 Complete the story with the correct form of the verbs.

Last Wednesday night, I ¹...**went**... (go) into town. My father ²..................... (take) me in his car and he ³..................... (say) he was coming to pick me up. I ⁴..................... (go) to the cinema and I ⁵..................... (watch) a film – it wasn't really very good. After the film, I ⁶..................... (wait) for my dad outside the cinema. It ⁷..................... (be) really cold!
Then my dad ⁸..................... (phone) me. He said: 'Sorry, I can't come. Catch the bus! See you later.'

But I ⁹..................... (not have) any money for the bus. So I ¹⁰..................... (start) to walk home. But then it ¹¹..................... (start) to rain. I ¹²..................... (get) very wet. So I ¹³..................... (stop) in the door of a bank.
Then I ¹⁴..................... (look) down at the floor – and I ¹⁵..................... (find) some money! There ¹⁶..................... (be) a two-pound coin on the ground. I ¹⁷..................... (pick) it up and ¹⁸..................... (run) to the bus stop. I ¹⁹..................... (catch) the last bus home. Lucky me!

5 Write about your 'perfect yesterday'.

....
....
....
....

And now go to the CD-ROM and do the Cartoon for Fun!

Past simple – negation

When you want to make a verb in the *past simple* negative, you use **didn't** (= **did not**) and the base form of the verb.

+	−
(work) I / you / he / she / it / we / they **worked**.	I / you / he / she / it / we / they **didn't work**.
(go) I / you / he / she / it / we / they **went** to school.	I / you / he / she / it / we / they **didn't go**.
(be) I / he / she / it **was** there.	I / he / she / it **wasn't** there.
you / we / they **were** there.	you / we / they **weren't** there.

1 Match the pictures and sentences.

1 We didn't enjoy our holiday last year.
2 The weather wasn't nice at all.
3 We didn't like the hotel.
4 The food wasn't very good.
5 The room was noisy so we didn't sleep well.
6 My mother didn't like the shops.
7 Dad and I didn't see the football match.
8 The good thing was – we went home after three days!

2 Write the phrases in the correct places.

asked
didn't ask
went
didn't go
saw
didn't see
~~worked~~
didn't work

1 My dad *worked* very hard yesterday, so when he came home he was very tired.
2 I didn't know the answer to the questions, so I phoned my friend Gill and .... her to help me.
3 Last year we went to New York – and I .... lots of famous people!
4 We .... to the cinema last night – the film was great!
5 The question was very difficult, so I was happy that the teacher .... me to answer it!
6 I .... on Friday night or Saturday, so I had to do all my homework on Sunday night.
7 I was really ill on Friday, so I .... to school.
8 A Was John at school yesterday? B I'm not sure – I .... him.

And now go to the CD-ROM and do the *Cartoon for Fun!*

Past simple – questions

Hello! See me on the CD-ROM to discover more about *past simple – questions* and to learn better when to use them.

When you want to make a question using the *past simple* of a verb, you use **did** + subject + the base form of the verb.

Statement	Question
(work) I / you / he / she / it / we / they **worked**.	**Did** I / you / he / she / it / we / they **work**?
(go) I / you / he / she / it / we / they **went** to school.	**Did** I / you / he / she / it / we / they **go** to school?
(be) I / he / she / it **was** there.	**Was** I / he / she / it there?
you / we / they **were** there.	**Were** you / we / they there?

1 Put the words in the correct order to make the questions. Then match them to the answers.

1 your / Was / good / holiday?
   Was your holiday good?
2 brother and sister / your / with / go / Did / you?
   ....
3 hotel / you / in / Did / a / stay?
   ....
4 own / you / food / cook / your / Did?
   ....

☐ Sometimes – but we went to restaurants too.
[1] Yes, it was great, thanks!
☐ No, I went with some friends.
☐ No, we didn't. We went camping.

2 Write the questions and the answers. Use the verbs in the box.

go
~~see~~
watch
do

1 A ......*Did*...... you ......*see*...... Annie yesterday?
   B No, I .... Annie – but I saw Julia.
2 A .... you .... to Italy on holiday?
   B No, we .... to Italy – we went to Spain.
3 A .... you .... the Maths homework last night?
   B Yes, I did – but I .... the French homework.
4 A .... you .... the football match last night?
   B No, I .... the football – I watched the science fiction film.

3 Complete the questions. Then answer them for you.

1 you / go / town / yesterday?
   Did you go to town yesterday?
   Yes, I did. / No, I didn't.
2 you / see / friends / last Saturday?
   ....
   ....
3 the teacher / give you / homework / last night?
   ....
   ....
4 your parents / go out / last weekend?
   ....
   ....

And now go to the CD-ROM and do the **Cartoon for Fun!**

Past simple – negation and questions

1 Put the dialogue in the correct order.

- [ ] **A** Which friends? Jimmy Hardy?
- [ ] **A** You walked around the shopping centre?
- [ ] **A** The shopping centre? Did you buy anything?
- [1] **A** So where did you go last night?
- [ ] **A** I just want to know what to give you for breakfast!
- [ ] **A** No food? Hmm – so are you hungry this morning?
- [ ] **B** I went to the shopping centre.
- [ ] **B** No – I didn't meet Jimmy, I met Andy and Jack. We didn't do much – we just walked around.
- [ ] **B** Yes, because we didn't have any money. So we couldn't buy anything and we didn't eat any food.
- [ ] **B** Yes, I'm very hungry! But mum – why all these questions?
- [ ] **B** No, I didn't go shopping – I just met my friends.

2 Circle the correct options.

1 … out last Saturday night?
   a You went   **b Did you go**   c Go you

2 … you in town yesterday?
   a Was   b Are   c Were

3 We went to the cinema, but we … the film.
   a not liked   b did like not   c didn't like

4 I phoned Johnny, but he … at home.
   a wasn't   b weren't   c didn't be

3 Complete the dialogue. Put the verbs into the correct form.

A Where ¹....did you go...... (go) last night?
B To the cinema.
A Who ²................ you .... (go) with?
B I went with Paula. I invited Ashley – but Ashley ³................ (not come).
A Oh dear. Well – what ⁴................ (be) the film like?
B The film ⁵................ (not be) very good. I ⁶................ (not like) it. But there was one good thing: I ⁷................ (not pay).
A You didn't pay?
B No. I ⁸................ (not have) any money. Paula paid.
A Oh. Where ⁹................ you .... (go) after the cinema?
B We went to a pizza place – but I ¹⁰................ (not be) hungry, so I ¹¹................ (not eat) anything. Paula ¹²................ (not have) anything, either.
A What ¹³................ you .... (talk) about?
B We ¹⁴................ (not talk) about anything. I ¹⁵................ (not want) to talk to Paula.
A It sounds like a wonderful evening.
B It ¹⁶................ (not be) a wonderful evening. It was terrible!
A I know – I was joking!

And now go to the CD-ROM and do the *Cartoon for Fun!*

Past time expressions

Use the *past simple* to tell a story. Add past time expressions, such as **a week ago**, **one day**, **the next day**, **then**, **later**, **after some time**, **finally**.

1 Complete the words in the sentences.

1 We did some shopping and had a coffee.
   T h e n we went home.
2 My uncle's staying with us. He arrived three days a _ _ .
3 We sat down in the cinema and two minutes l _ _ _ _ the film started.
4 The film was awful! A _ _ _ _ half an hour, we left.
5 Last summer we were in Italy. O _ _ day, we went to Venice.
   The n _ _ _ day, we visited Padua.
6 I waited for Julie for an hour. F _ _ _ _ _ _ , she arrived and said she was sorry.

2 Complete the text with the words in the box.

ten minutes later
One day
~~Two years ago~~
The next day
finally
After thirty minutes

¹...... *Two years ago* ......, my family (my mum and dad, my little brother Jeremy and me) went on holiday to London. ².., we went out to look in some shops. We went to Oxford Street and started walking around. There were hundreds of people everywhere. Suddenly, my mum asked: 'Where's Jeremy?' Well, we looked everywhere for him but we couldn't find him. ³.., my dad said: 'I'm going to the police.' So we all went to the police station. We walked in, and my dad started to say what the problem was. My mum was really worried – but, ⁴.., a policewoman came in and she was holding Jeremy's hand. 'We found him in a toyshop,' the policewoman said. Mum was so happy! I was happy too, because ⁵.. we could go and finish our shopping!

⁶.., Jeremy said 'Let's go shopping again.' My parents just said: 'Noooo!!'

And now go to the CD-ROM and do the **Cartoon for Fun!**

Comparatives

All one-syllable adjectives, and most two-syllable adjectives, form the comparative with **–er** and the superlative with **–est**. Other two-syllable adjectives and all other adjectives form the comparative with **more** and the superlative with **most**.

Be careful with spelling: sometimes the final letter (**g**, **t**, etc) is doubled; **y** at the end of an adjective becomes **i**.

The comparatives of **good** and **bad** are irregular: **better**, **worse**.

I'm old**er than** my brother.
I'm big**ger than** my sister.
I'm heav**ier than** my mum.
I'm **more** intelligent **than** my dad.
I'm **better** at maths **than** you.

1 Read the sentences and tick the one that is correct.

1 My pencil is longer than your pencil.

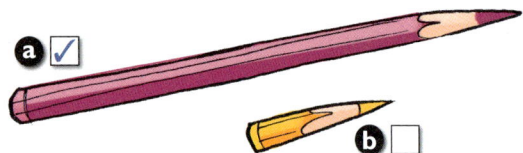

2 My school bag is heavier than your school bag.

3 My dog is more intelligent than your dog.

4 My pet is more exotic than your pet.

5 My cat is prettier than your cat.

His game console is more popular than my game console.

7 My bike is faster than your bike.

8 My watch is more expensive than your watch.

2 Underline the correct words.

1 This table is really <u>heavy</u> / heavier. Can you help me?
2 I'm three days old / older than you.
3 The film is good / better than the book.
4 That snake looks dangerous / more dangerous than the other one.
5 The waves are always small here. It's a very safe / safer beach.
6 It was cold / colder yesterday than it is today.
7 Oliver is really intelligent / more intelligent. He always gets the best marks.
8 I was a very ugly / uglier baby, but look at me now!

3 Complete the sentences using the same adjective.

1 Cape Town is beautiful but Rio de Janeiro is ...*more beautiful*... .
2 Cheetahs are fast but antelopes are ....
3 Kate Pimm is popular but Debbie Helps is ....
4 Porsches are expensive but Ferraris are ....
5 Chimpanzees are intelligent but dolphins are ....
6 My first girlfriend was pretty but my new girlfriend is ....
7 Your problem is big but my problem is ....
8 That spider is poisonous but this one is ....

4 Complete the poem with the comparative form of the adjectives.

My perfect cousin (a love poem)

I'm ¹............................... (old) than him but he's ²............................... (tall) than me
(I'm one metre forty, he's one forty-three.)

I hate to say it but he's ³............................... (intelligent) than me
His last grade was A and my grade was C!

The girls all say he's ⁴............................... (handsome) than me.
(But I think he looks like an old chimpanzee!)

I think he must be ⁵............................... (friendly) than me.
He's got hundreds of friends. I've only got three!

He's got lots of money. He's ⁶............................... (rich) than me.
He's got an amazing new bike and a brand new TV.

He loves all sports and he's ⁷............................... (good) than me.
He's ⁸............................... (strong) and ⁹............................... (fast) and eats salad for tea!

Yes, he's got everything and he's great, my cousin Jim.
But with you by my side, I'm ¹⁰............................... (happy) than him.

And now go to the CD-ROM and do the *Cartoon for Fun!*

Superlatives

You use the superlative form of an adjective to talk about things which are extreme in a group. Add the word **the**. Again, be careful with the spelling.

The superlatives of **good** and **bad** are irregular: **the best**, **the worst**.

I'm **the** old**est** in the class.
It's **the** big**gest** animal in the world.
She's **the** prett**iest** girl in the school.
He's **the most** intelligent person I know.

1 Complete the table.

adjective	comparative	superlative
old	older than	
new		
tall		
hot		the hottest
big		
pretty		
heavy	heavier than	
important		
boring		
relaxing		the most relaxing
good		
bad		

2 Use phrases from 1 to complete the sentences.

It was Sunday and it was 42°C. It was ⁱ......the hottest...... day of the year! My school books were on the table in front of me. I had my final tests next week – ²................................ tests of the year! Fail and spend your summer holiday studying. I wanted to go to the beach. I looked at my books. 'Why is studying so boring? It's even ³................................ doing housework.' I thought. The phone rang. It was Diana Nicholls. Beautiful Diana Nicholls –

⁴................................ girl in the school! What did she want with me? She wanted me to go to the beach. 'But the tests …?' I asked her.
'The tests!' she said. 'You need to relax. A day on the beach is ⁵................................ studying.' It was a good idea. In fact it was ⁶................................ idea of the day. 'OK.' I said. I had a great time on the beach. It was definitely ⁷................................ studying at home.

And the tests? My grades were bad. Really bad. They were ⁸................................ in the school.
Tomorrow is the first day of the summer holiday. Three weeks of studying for me. But that's no problem. The weather is cold (only 23° C) and my new girlfriend is going to study with me – Diana. Her grades were terrible too.

3 Read about the four spies and put the symbols in the correct spaces in the table.

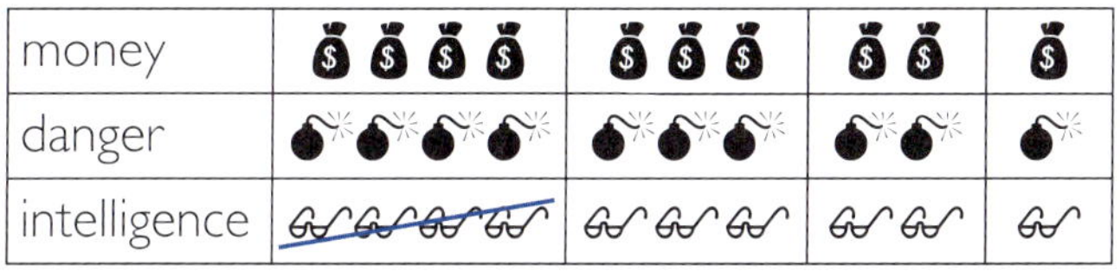

money	💰💰💰💰	💰💰💰	💰💰	💰
danger	💣💣💣💣	💣💣💣	💣💣	💣
intelligence	〰️〰️〰️〰️	〰️〰️〰️	〰️〰️	〰️

Dick Spyder — **Raymond Black** — **Edgar Peril** — **Lucy Diamond**

money
danger
intelligence

1 Edgar Peril is more intelligent than Raymond Black but he isn't as intelligent as Dick Spyder.
2 Lucy Diamond is richer than Edgar Peril.
3 Raymond Black is the second most dangerous.
4 Dick Spyder isn't as rich as Edgar Peril.
5 Edgar Peril is more dangerous than Raymond Black.
6 Lucy Diamond is the most intelligent.
7 Raymond Black is the richest.
8 Lucy Diamond isn't as dangerous as Dick Spyder.

4 Look at the completed table in ③ and complete the sentences.

1 Dick Spyder ...*isn't as rich as*... Edgar Peril. (rich)
2 Lucy Diamond .... Dick Spyder. (intelligent)
3 Raymond Black .... Edgar Peril. (dangerous)
4 Dick Spyder .... Raymond Black. (intelligent)
5 Lucy Diamond .... Dick Spyder. (rich)
6 Raymond Black .... Lucy Diamond. (intelligent)
7 Edgar Peril .... (dangerous)
8 Raymond Black .... (rich)

5 Put the words in order.

Eight things you never knew about my family:

1 mum / than / taller / my / I'm (but don't tell her)
   I'm taller than my mum.

2 funniest / the / in / person / family / my / I'm
   ....

3 pretty / as / I'm / my / mum / as
   ....

4 older / than / dog / is / me / our (by two weeks!)
   ....

5 as / my / intelligent / me / sister / isn't / as (but she thinks she is)
   ....

6 brother / my / is / me / youngest / than / older (it's possible — think about it)
   ....

7 thinks / isn't / funny / as / as / my / dad / he
   ....

8 but / richest / meanest / dad / is / the / my / he's / also / the
   ....

6 Write six similar facts about your family.

as ... as

This is how you can talk about things that are similar or not similar.

I'm **as** tall **as** you = We're the same height.

I'm **not as** tall **as** you. = You're taller than me.

1 Read the information card and write T (*True*) or F (*False*) for the sentences.

	T Rex	Stegosaurus	Triceratops
Height	5.6 m	3 m	3 m
Weight	6000 kg	3100 kg	5500 kg
Danger rating	9	2	2
Intelligence rating	8	1	8

1 The Stegosaurus was not as dangerous as the T Rex. **T**
2 The Triceratops was as tall as the Stegosaurus.
3 The T Rex was as intelligent as the Stegosaurus.
4 The Triceratops was not as heavy as the T Rex.
5 The T Rex was not as dangerous as the Stegosaurus.
6 The Stegosaurus was not as tall as the T Rex.
7 The Stegosaurus was as heavy as the T Rex.
8 The Stegosaurus was not as dangerous as the Triceratops.

2 Using the information in **1** write *(not) as ... as* sentences to compare:

1 Stegosaurus / T Rex (height) *The Stegosaurus was not as tall as the T Rex.*
2 Triceratops / T Rex (intelligence) ....
3 Triceratops / Stegosaurus (height) ....
4 Triceratops / T Rex (danger) ....

3 Rewrite the sentences using *(not) as ... as* sentences.

1 I'm taller than my mum. *My mum's not as tall as me.*
2 The film is funnier than the book. ....
3 Mr Brown is more popular than Mr Thomas. ....
4 Maths is more difficult than English. ....
5 Your present was more expensive than my present. ....
6 Football is more exciting than tennis. ....

And now go to the CD-ROM and do the

why / because

The word **why?** is used to ask for a reason. The word **because** is used when you answer a question that begins with **why**.

1 Match the jokes and the answers.

❶ Why didn't the skeleton go to the party?

❷ Why is 6 scared of 7?

❸ Why is V a monster?

❹ Why was the computer cold?

❺ Why do birds sit on their eggs?

❻ Why did the Maths book cry?

❼ Why do you go to bed every night?

❽ Why did the elephant wear red shoes?

❾ Why do birds fly south in the winter?

a Because it always comes after U. ◯
b Because it didn't close its windows. ◯
c Because it's too far to walk. ◯
d Because the bed doesn't come to you. ◯
e Because they don't have chairs. ◯
f Because his white ones were dirty. ◯
g Because 7 ate 9. ◯
h Because he had no body to go with. ◯
i Because it had so many problems. ◯

And now go to the CD-ROM and do the **Cartoon for Fun!**

21

Directions (prepositions of place)

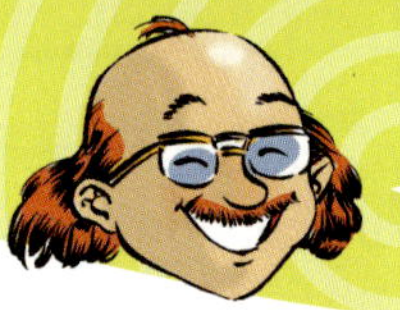

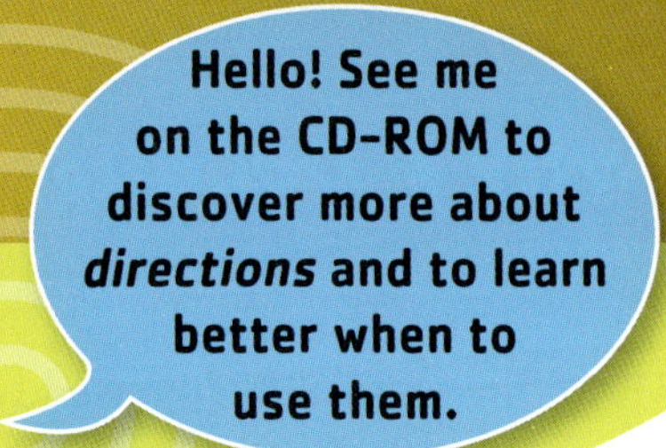

> Hello! See me on the CD-ROM to discover more about *directions* and to learn better when to use them.

1 Write the words / phrases under the pictures.

behind
in front of
~~next to~~
opposite
on the corner
round the

1. next to

2. ....

3. ....

4. ....

5. ....

6. ....

2 Write the words in the correct order.

1 the / on / it's / corner
   It's on the corner.

2 corner / go / round / the
   ....

3 ahead / straight / go
   ....

4 it's / front / bank / of / the / in
   ....

5 next / the / it's / to / supermarket
   ....

6 take / right / the / first
   ....

7 second / the / take / left
   ....

3 Look at the map on page 23. Read the directions. Write the place you get to.

1 Go straight ahead. Take the first right. Go to the end of Queen Street. It's opposite the bank.
   restaurant

2 Go straight ahead. Take the second left. Walk about 100 metres. It's next to the music shop.
   ....

3 Go straight ahead. Take the third right. Go past the park. It's on your left.
   ....

4 Go straight ahead. Take the first left. Go to the end of the street. It's on the corner of West Street — opposite the chemist's.
   ....

5 Go straight ahead. Take the third left. It's at the end of the street — on the right, opposite the supermarket.
   ....

6 Go straight ahead. Take the second right. Go past the bank. Turn left. It's on your right.
   ....

4. **Write directions for someone to get to the following places. Start from the bottom of High Street – the same as in 3.**

1 The restaurant in King Street: ....
....

2 The railway station: ....
....

3 The tourist office: ....
....

4 The café in Abbey Street: ....
....

5 The post office in North Street: ....
....

6 The bus station: ....
....

And now go to the CD-ROM and do the *Cartoon for Fun!*

going to (revision)

Do you remember? To talk about plans and intentions for the future we use **am / is / are** + **going to** + base form of the verb.
We use **going to** also to say that something is about to happen.

I'm		buy a new phone.
You're		like that video.
He's / She's / It's	going to	go away.
We're		learn a new language.
You're		play together.
They're		get a dog.

1 Match the sentences with the people.

1 I'm going to send the bill to your mum.
2 Watch out! It's going to fly away!
3 What am I going to tell the teacher?
4 We're going to play computer games.
5 Is she going to wear that?
6 I'm going to go home.
7 I'm going to kill the dragon.
8 We're going to make pizza.
9 When is he going to stop?
10 Who's going to go for a walk?

going to – negative

To make the negative form of **going to** use **'m not / isn't / aren't** + **going to** + base form of the verb.

I**'m not going to** help you.
You **aren't going to** like this.
He/She **isn't going to** watch TV all day.
It **isn't going to** rain tomorrow.
We **aren't going to** tell anybody.
They **aren't going to** play football this afternoon.

1 Complete the horoscope with the words in the box.

| going to meet | going to be | ~~going to get~~ | going to have |
| going to ask | going to fight | going to cook | going to give |

Aries

April is going to be a fantastic month:

1 You're ....*going to get*.... the best grade in the test.
2 Your mum's .... your favourite dinner every day.
3 You're .... very popular with your classmates.
4 You're .... a new 'special' friend.
5 Your teacher isn't .... you any homework.
6 Your mum and dad aren't .... you to help in the house.
7 Your brothers and sisters aren't .... with you all day.
8 And you aren't .... any problems all month.

2 Underline the correct options.

Did you have a great April? Good – because May is going to be terrible!

1 *It's / It isn't* going to rain all month.
2 *You're / You aren't* going to fall off your bike – twice!
3 Your teacher *is / isn't* going to tell you off all the time.
4 Your dad *is / isn't* going to give you any pocket money.
5 Your brothers *are / aren't* going to break your computer.
6 Your friends *are / aren't* going to invite you to their party.
7 *You're / You aren't* going to be sad for 30 days.
8 Because, *you're / you aren't* going to have any fun for a month.

And now go to the CD-ROM and do the **Cartoon for Fun!**

might (not)

Hello! See me on the CD-ROM to discover more about *might (not)* and to learn better when to use it.

To talk about future possibility, use **might / might not** and the base form of the verb.

I/you/he/she/we/they **might** go to the cinema tonight.
I/you/he/she/we/they **might not** like the film.
It **might** rain tonight.
It **might not** rain tomorrow.

1 Write the sentences in the speech bubbles.

You might not have enough money.

It might rain.

Your teachers might not like it.

I might not have any more children.

You might have an accident.

You might get hungry.

1 ....

2 ....

3 ....

4 ....

5 ....

6 ....

2 Complete the dialogue with *might* or *might not*.

Bob What's the matter William? Are you worried?
William I've got a job interview at three o'clock in town.
Bob So what's the problem?
William I don't know how to get there.
Bob Well, it's only one o'clock. Why don't you walk?
William I ¹...*might*... get too tired. And then I ².................... understand the questions in the interview.
Bob OK. Get a taxi.
William It ³.................... be too expensive. I've only got £5 and that ⁴.................... be enough.
Bob I know. Go by bike.
William Oh no. I ⁵.................... get there.
Bob Why not?
William I ⁶.................... have an accident.
Bob OK, so take a bus.
William But I ⁷.................... get on the wrong bus and I ⁸.................... get lost.
Bob I give up. What kind of job is it anyway?
William It's to work with tourist information. Telling people where to go and how to get there.

26

3 **Match the sentences to the pictures.**

1 They might miss the plane.
2 They're going to watch James Bond tonight.
3 They're not going to watch James Bond tonight.
4 They might play tennis.
5 They're going to play tennis.
6 They're not going to play tennis.
7 They might watch James Bond tonight.
8 They're going to miss the plane.
9 They're not going to miss the plane.

4 **Complete the sentences with *might*, *be going to* or *not be going to*.**

1 The station is 5 km from here so ....*we're going to*.......... take a taxi. It's too far to walk and there's no bus.
2 We .... see an opera tonight. I bought the tickets yesterday.
3 I .... buy the red dress or I .... buy the blue one. I can't decide.
4 Jim doesn't eat meat so I'm .... cook steak for them.
5 The children .... sleep at a friend's house this Friday. Great — peace and quiet for us!
6 We .... go to the party. There's a 50% chance.
7 Mum hates loud music so she's .... like this punk CD.
8 We .... have another one. Five children is enough!

5 **Write about some of your plans for the weekend.**

I'm going to ....
I'm not going to ....
I might ....
I'm going to ....
I'm not going to ....
I might ....

And now go to the CD-ROM and do the *Cartoon for Fun!*

Present continuous for future

To talk about plans and arrangements already made for the future, use the *present continuous*. Often there is a future time expression like *tomorrow*, *next weekend*, *next week*.

What **are you doing** tomorrow?
I'm going to Sam's party.
She's leaving for Italy on Saturday.
We're taking our exams next year.

1 Complete the first part of the sentences with the verbs in the box.

'm not taking
're meeting
're visiting
's competing
're moving
's getting
isn't having
's seeing

1 We .... New York ....
2 He .... a party ....
3 They .... to France ....
4 She .... in the Olympics ....
5 She .... married ....
6 I .... the maths exam ....
7 He .... the dentist ....
8 We .... at the cinema ....

2 Match the sentences in **1** to the pictures and complete them with the time expressions.

a
in September

b
for his birthday

c
next year

d
next week

e
this afternoon

f
on Monday

g
at seven o'clock

h
tomorrow

28

3 **Next week there is no school. You have already decided what to do. Look at your diary and answer the questions.**

1 What are you doing on Monday?
   ....
2 When are you going swimming?
   ....
3 Are you going on your bike ride alone?
   ....
4 Where are you having a picnic?
   ....
5 What are you doing at the Computer Crazy Club?
   ....
6 What are you doing at the weekend?
   ....
7 Who are you going with?
   ....
8 Are you travelling alone?
   ....
9 Are you travelling by train?
   ....
10 When are you coming back?
   ....

Monday
play football with friends
Tuesday
go to the swimming pool with Sara
Wednesday
bike ride and picnic in the country with Peter
Thursday
meet friends at the Computer Crazy Club
Friday
fly to Edinburgh with my family
Saturday
visit Edinburgh Castle
Sunday
fly back home in the evening

4 **Josh is going on holiday. Ask him about his plans.**

1 (where go)
   Where are you going?
2 (when go)
   ....
3 (travel by car)
   ....
4 (go alone)
   ....
5 (where stay)
   ....

6 (how long stay)
   ....
7 (what do)
   ....
8 (what see)
   ....
9 (who visit)
   ....
10 (when return)
   ....

5 **Imagine you are Josh. Answer the questions in 4 about you.**

will – future

You can use the **will**-future for predictions, decisions at the time of speaking, and promises.

I'll (= I **will**) **see** you tomorrow.	It **won't** (= It **will not**) **rain** tomorrow.
We'll come (= We **will come**) to see you.	He **won't** (= He **will not**) **know** the answer.
You'll (= You **will**) **enjoy** it.	They **won't** (= They **will not**) **go** to Italy.

1 Write the short forms.

1 It will be sunny tomorrow.
   It'll be sunny tomorrow.
2 I will not be late.
   ....
3 There will not be any fog.
   ....
4 My father will come and pick us up.
   ....
5 The rain will stop soon.
   ....
6 I will not come to your house tomorrow.
   ....

2 Complete the sentences with *will* or *won't* and a verb from the box.

~~not come~~
not bite
like
be
rain
not sleep
not be
go

1 Don't invite Jim to your party – he hates parties, so he ......*won't come*...... .
2 There are some big clouds in the sky – I think it .... this afternoon.
3 Eat some more, or you .... hungry at 10 o'clock.
4 I don't feel very well. I think I .... to the doctor tomorrow.
5 My dog's really friendly – don't worry, he .... you!
6 I'm going to buy this CD for my mum's birthday – I'm sure she .... it!
7 You didn't do your homework?! Well, the teacher .... happy about that!
8 Don't drink coffee! It's 11 o'clock at night – you .... well.

3 Match the sentences from **2** with the pictures.

4 Write what the people think they *will / won't* do next weekend.

1 Paul thinks *he'll do his homework* on Sunday.
2 Susan thinks .... Jenny on Friday night.
3 My dad thinks .... on Sunday morning.
4 My mum thinks .... on Saturday.
5 My brother thinks .... on Saturday morning.
6 I think .... on Sunday night!

5 Complete the text. Use *'ll or won't* and the verbs.

What can I do on Saturday night? Well, perhaps I ¹ *'ll go* (go) to Jane's party. Hmmm – but I ² .... (not know) anyone at her party, so it ³ .... (not be) fun. OK – I ⁴ .... (phone) Sam. I'm sure he ⁵ .... (have) ideas about what we can do. Oh no! Sam's in London. OK – I ⁶ .... (invite) Alison to the cinema. Oh – I forgot. We had an argument and we're not friends any more, so she certainly ⁷ .... (not come).
OK – perhaps I ⁸ .... (stay) at home and do my homework. It ⁹ .... (not kill) me!

6 Complete the sentences. Use *'ll or won't* and a verb from the box.

~~become~~
have
not have
be
get
take
live
send

When I leave school ...
1 I *'ll become* a famous footballer.
2 I .... incredibly rich!
3 I .... in a really, really big house!
4 I .... married.
5 I .... six children.
6 I .... my family on holiday every year to Australia and the USA.
7 I .... all my children to university.
8 ... and then: I .... any money any more!!

7 Write six sentences about <u>you</u> when you leave school. What will/won't you do?

And now go to the CD-ROM and do the *Cartoon for Fun!*

31

can for permission

Use **Can I** / **Can we** to ask for permission.

Can I go to the bathroom?

Can we open the window?

1 Match the pictures and the sentences.

1 Rick, can I come in?
2 Mum, can we go for a swim?
3 We can't watch TV, we can't play games, we can't move, what can we do?
4 Can I say something?
5 Dad, can I give Fluffy some ice cream?
6 Can I buy some new shorts?
7 Can we go on the roller-coaster?
8 Can I go out with Josh tonight?

2 Complete the sentences with the words in the box.

Can I watch TV now?
Can we stay at home?
Can I stop now?
Can I have another slice of cake?
Can we play hide-and-seek?
Can I see them?

1 I'm tired. ....
2 Where are your exam results? ....
3 We don't want to go to granny. ....
4 .... It's time for the children's programmes.
5 .... It's delicious.
6 Helen is coming to play. ....

3 Put the words in order to make requests for permission.

1 I / go / tonight / can / out / ?
   Can I go out tonight?
2 open / I / can / presents / my / ?
   ....
3 we / play / in the garden / football / can / ?
   ....
4 can / our / we / tomorrow / tidy / rooms / ?
   ....
5 I / can / your / borrow / mobile / today / ?
   ....
6 use / dad's / now / I / computer / can / ?
   ....
7 can / the / I / trip / school / on / go / ?
   ....
8 invite / can / I / friends / my / stay / to / ?
   ....

4 Permission or ability? Write P or A.

1 Can I stay at Belinda's house tonight? ....
2 I can't ride this bike. ....
3 Can you swim 100 metres? ....
4 I can't speak Spanish. ....
5 Can I phone aunt Joan? ....
6 Can we go shopping? ....

should / shouldn't

Hello! See me on the CD-ROM to discover more about *should / shouldn't* and to learn better when to use them.

When you want to say that it is a good idea (or not) for someone to do something, you can use **should / shouldn't** (= **should not**) and the base form of the verb.

You **should do** some exercise.   You **shouldn't eat** so quickly.
We **should** go home now.   They **shouldn't make** so much noise.

1   Match the pictures and sentences.

1   It's late. We should go home now.
2   You shouldn't eat so quickly.
3   They shouldn't make so much noise.
4   He should be careful.
5   Perhaps you should wash him.
6   You shouldn't look at my work.
7   We should call the police.
8   It's great — you should go and see it.
9   She shouldn't go to school for a few days.

2   Complete the dialogues. Use *should* or *shouldn't* and a phrase from the box.

charge it more often
go later
~~eat an apple~~
stay out late
go to bed early
call him bad names
worry so much
have a party

1   **A** I'm feeling really hungry.
    B Well, perhaps you *should eat an apple* or something.
2   **A** I've got an important test tomorrow.
    B Really? Well then, you .... and get some good sleep.
3   **A** I think Paul's angry with me.
    B Of course he is! You really .... you know.
4   **A** I heard a noise! Perhaps it's a ghost.
    B Don't be silly. You ....
5   **A** I'm sorry I didn't phone you. The battery in my mobile was flat.
    B You always say that! You know, I think you ....
6   **A** I'm going to be fifteen on Saturday.
    B Great! We .... How about Sunday at my place?
7   **A** I want to go to the park and play football.
    B Well, it's raining, so I think you ....
8   **A** I was really tired on Monday morning.
    B It's not surprising. You .... on Sunday nights!

3 Put the words in the correct order to make the sentences.

1 home / You / at night / alone / shouldn't / walk
   You shouldn't walk home alone at night.

2 sorry / you're / You / say / should
   ....

3 any / shouldn't / make / We / noise
   ....

4 dog / take / We / for a walk / should / this afternoon / the
   ....

5 shouldn't / so / I / eat / chocolate / much
   ....

6 invite / cinema / We / should / the / to / him
   ....

4 Which sentence from **3** goes with each picture? Write numbers.

5 Complete the sentences with *should / shouldn't* and your own ideas.

I think that in school we ....

My friend is very tired. Perhaps he/she ....

I think my parents ....

I want to be successful when I'm older. Perhaps I ....

....

The authorities in our town ....

....

And now go to the CD-ROM and do the *Cartoon for Fun!*

35

have to / don't have to

Hello! See me on the CD-ROM to discover more about *have to / don't have to* and to learn better when to use them.

Use **have to** to talk about an obligation.
Use **don't have to** to talk about no obligation.

I / you / we / they **have to go** now.　　I / you / we / they **don't have to wear** a uniform.
He / she / it **has to be** good.　　He / she / it **doesn't have to work**.

1 Match the sentences and the signs.

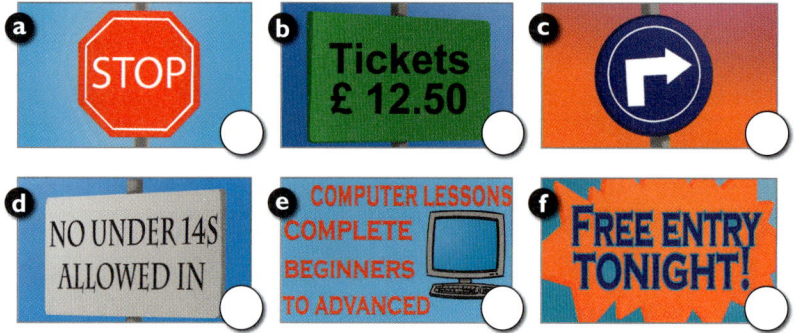

1 You have to turn right here.
2 You don't have to pay to go in.
3 You have to be over 14.
4 You have to stop.
5 You have to pay to go in.
6 You don't have to know anything.

2 Write the words in the correct order.

1 up / I / to / get / have / on weekdays / early
   I have to get up early on weekdays.
2 to / party / You / come / to / my / have
   ....
3 My / have / study / doesn't / hard / brother / to
   ....
4 for homework / has / She / write / to / a / story
   ....

5 have / go / tomorrow / We / don't / to / school / to
   ....
6 every weekend / my / have / to / I / tidy / room
   ....
7 do / don't / We / have / washing up / to / the
   ....
8 you / wear / have / school / Do / a / to / uniform / to
   ....?

3 Match the sentences to make mini-dialogues.

1 Do you have to do homework every night?
2 Can you help me, please?
3 I don't want any breakfast, thanks.
4 Can I borrow your bike?
5 There's a free concert in the park.
6 Why can't I see this film?
7 I don't have to get up early tomorrow.
8 Your trainers are really old!

a OK – but you have to bring it back at 5.00.
b Why? Is it a holiday or something?
c No – I only have to do it on Fridays.
d Yes – I have to buy some new ones.
e Because you have to be over 14 to watch it.
f But you have to eat something before school!
g Sorry, no – I have to go out now.
h Great – so we don't have to pay!

4 Complete the text with the phrases in the box.

Life at the Milky Way School for Martians

don't have to be
don't have to take
don't have to switch
don't have to work
have to leave
have to wave
have to talk
~~have to wear~~
have to use
have to wiggle

At our school, we ¹ *have to wear* a uniform – it's green and black and pink, our favourite colours! We go to school at 6 o'clock in the morning, and we ² .... at 7 o'clock at night. We ³ .... our mobile phones off – in fact, we ⁴ .... our phones every 30 minutes, and we ⁵ .... very loudly, too. The school gives us 5 kilos of broccoli to eat in the break so we ⁶ .... our own food to school. When a teacher comes into the classroom, we ⁷ .... our arms around (all ten of them) and we ⁸ .... our ears (all six of them) – boring! Our favourite teacher is Mrs Gorgly – in her lessons, we ⁹ .... hard and we ¹⁰ .... quiet, either!

5 Look at the table. Write sentences about the people.

	Angus	Becky	Colin and Sally
wear a school uniform	✓	✗	✓
help with the housework	✗	✗	✓
study hard before a test	✓	✓	✗
leave home early to go to school	✗	✓	✗

1 Angus *has to wear a school uniform.*
2 Angus *doesn't have to help with the housework.*
3 Angus ....
4 Angus ....
5 Becky ....
6 Becky ....
7 Becky ....
8 Becky ....
9 Colin and Sally ....
10 Colin and Sally ....
11 Colin and Sally ....
12 Colin and Sally ....

6 Now write sentences about YOU. Write about the activities in **5**.

I .... a school uniform.
I .... with the housework.
I ....
I ....

And now go to the CD-ROM and do the *Cartoon for Fun!*

must / mustn't

Hello! See me on the CD-ROM to discover more about *must / mustn't* and to learn better when to use them.

Use **must** to talk about an obligation.
Use **mustn't** to talk about a prohibition.

You **must be** home before ten.
I **mustn't be** late for school.
We **must switch** our phones off.
You **mustn't feed** the animals in the zoo.

1 Match the person and the things he/she says.

1 You mustn't feed the animals.
2 You mustn't come home late.
3 You mustn't walk on the grass.
4 You must be quiet in here.
5 You must clean your teeth two or three times a day.
6 You must eat fruit and vegetables.

a doctor
b librarian
c dentist
d zoo-keeper
e park-keeper
f parent

2 Complete the sentences.

The Wannagobak campsite has lots of rules. Here they are:

1 You ...*mustn't play*... loud music.
2 You .... at 6 o'clock.
3 You .... your clothes on the tent-ropes.
4 You .... on the campsite.
5 You .... at 10 o'clock.
6 You .... the campsite.

3 Complete the sentences. Use *must* or *mustn't* and a verb from the box.

~~be~~
eat
climb
be
jump
put
wear
touch

1 The baby's asleep, so you ...*must be*... quiet, OK?
2 Come on — it's 8.30 already. We .... late for school again!
3 It's an important day, so you .... your best clothes.
4 Your shoes are very dirty — you .... them on the chairs.
5 Hamburgers aren't good for you, so you .... too many.
6 Now remember — in the museum, you can look but you .... anything!
7 An important rule in the swimming pool is — you .... into the pool.
8 Snowy — you silly cat! You .... trees if you can't get down again!

4 *Must* or *mustn't*? Complete the rules for this English school.

1 You .... wear a school uniform.
2 You .... do your homework every day.
3 You .... bring your mobile phone to school.
4 You .... listen to the teacher.
5 You .... listen to your MP3 player.
6 You .... eat in the classroom.
7 You .... run in the corridors.
8 You .... ask for permission to go to the bathroom.

5 What are the rules in YOUR school? Complete the sentences.

Clothes
1 We must ....
2 We mustn't ....

Homework
3 We must ....
4 We mustn't ....

Behaviour in class
5 We must ....
6 We mustn't ....

Phone and gadgets
7 We must ....
8 We mustn't ....

And now go to the CD–ROM and do the *Cartoon for Fun!*

Shall we ... ? / How / What about ... ?

Do you remember? You use **Let's** to suggest doing something with other people. You can also use:
Shall we + base form + ?
How about + –ing form + ?
What about + –ing form + ?

Let's go for walk.
Shall we go to the beach?
How about going to the park?
What about going to the circus?

1 Reorder the words to make suggestions.

1 away / shall / run / we / ?
....

2 dinner / about / making / how / ?
....

3 nice / read / a / shall / story / we / ?
....

4 song / sing / best / let's / our / !
....

5 up / the / cleaning / about / garage / what / ?
....

6 walk / about / going / for / a / how / ?
....

2 Match the sentences in **1** to the pictures.

I'd prefer to … / I'd rather …

If you want to suggest something different you can say:

I'd prefer + **to** + base form
I'd rather + base form

A Shall we go shopping?
B I'd prefer to stay at home.
A Let's play tennis.
B I'd rather watch TV.

1 Write the alternative suggestions in the speech bubbles.

I'd prefer to build a house of bricks.

I'd rather watch *Shrek Forever After*.

I'd prefer to wait for a salsa.

I'd rather go to a cleaner place.

I'd prefer to play volleyball.

I'd rather eat home-made food.

a How about going to see *The Tree of Life*?

b Shall we build a house of straw or one of sticks?

c Let's land on the Moon.

d Shall we dance this waltz?

e How about going to a restaurant?

f Shall we go for a swim?

41

one – ones

> Hello! See me on the CD-ROM to discover more about *one – ones* and to learn better when to use them.

When you want to repeat a noun that you have already used in a sentence, you can replace it with **one** (singular) or **ones** (plural).

I don't like the green **T-shirt**.	I like the blue **one**.
Do you want the pink or blue **jeans**?	The blue **ones**.

1 Match the questions and answers.

1 Which pizza would you like?
2 Which gym do you go to?
3 Which film do you want to see?
4 Which films do you like best?
5 Which T-shirt do you want?
6 Which jeans do you want?
7 Which girls are your sisters?
8 Which girl is your sister?

a The ones wearing red shoes.
b The one in the High Street opposite the bank.
c The blue ones.
d The blue one.
e The one with ham and mushrooms on it.
f The one wearing red shoes.
g Ones with Brad Pitt in them!
h The one with Brad Pitt in it.

2 Complete the dialogues with *one* or *ones*.

1 **A** Would you like a sandwich?
   B Yes, please. .... with cheese

2 **A** Did you buy some jeans?
   B Yes, I bought the blue ....

3 **A** Did you watch that horror film?
   B No we watched a detective ....

4 **A** Did the robber take all the paintings?
   B No, just the .... in the library.

5 **A** Which boy hit you?
   B That .... in the green T-shirt.

6 **A** Do you like these shoes?
   B I like the green .... better.

3 Underline the correct words. A = Assistant, D = Dave.

A Hello, can I help you?
D Yes, I'd like to try on some sunglasses – the ¹one / <u>ones</u> over there in the window.
A These ²one / ones?
D No, the ³one / ones next to the green cap.
A Which ⁴one / ones? There are lots of green caps in the window.
D The ⁵one / ones with the red bit on it.
A This ⁶one / ones?
D No! No, not that ⁷one / ones, the red and green cap next to the sunglasses.
A This ⁸one / ones?
D Yes.
A And you want to try this ⁹one / ones on?
D No, I don't want to try a cap on. I want to try on the sunglasses. The ¹⁰one / ones next to that cap. 
A These ¹¹one / ones.
D Yes. Yes, those ¹²one / ones.
A I'm sorry. These sunglasses aren't for sale.

And now go to the CD-ROM and do the **Cartoon for Fun!**

Countable and uncountable nouns

Countable nouns have a singular and a plural form.

a dog – three dogs   an orange – two oranges

Uncountable nouns only have a singular form.

water   money

1 Look at the pictures and do the two crosswords.

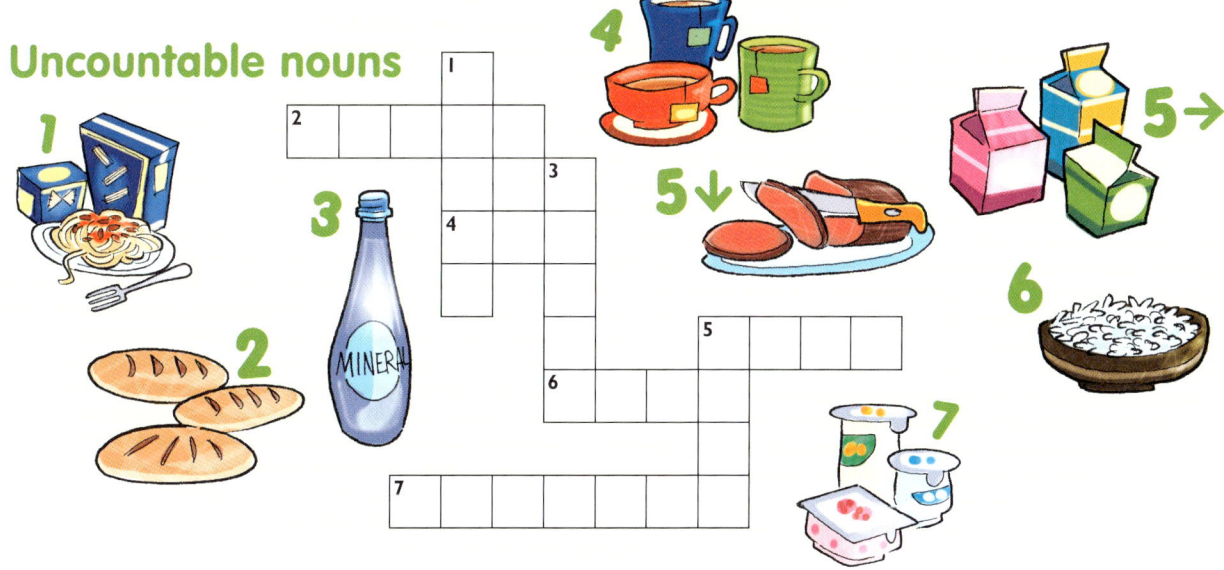

Countable nouns

Uncountable nouns

43

some / any

Use **some** to talk about things you cannot count, or if you don't know the number of the things. Use **any** to ask if something is there, or to say that something is not there.

some	any
We've got **some onions**.	We haven't got **any onions**.
I've got **some money**.	I haven't got **any money**.
Do you want **some potatoes**?	Is there **any milk** in the fridge?
Would you like **some soup**?	Have we got **any strawberries**?

1 Match the sentences / questions with the pictures.

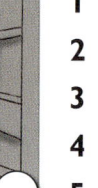

a b

1 Dad — can I have some money, please?
2 Mum — have we got any milk?
3 Mum — we need some ice cream.
4 No thanks — I don't want any ice cream.
5 Of course I can go out — I haven't got any work!
6 Sis — I need to buy something. Have you got any money?
7 Sorry, I can't go out — I've got to do some work.
8 Would you like some milk?

c d

e f g h

2 Match the sentences to make mini-dialogues.

1 We haven't got any chocolate.
2 Let's listen to some music.
3 Hello. Do you need any help?
4 I haven't got any ideas.
5 Have you got any pets at home?
6 Mum — we haven't got any toothpaste.
7 Please be quiet — I've got some work to do.
8 Oh no — there are some dogs in the street.

a Yes please — I want some information about buses.
b Look in the cupboard — there's some toothpaste in there.
c OK — I'm not going to make any noise.
d Yes we have — there's some in the kitchen.
e No — I'd prefer to watch some DVDs.
f Where? I can't see any dogs!
g No — mum doesn't want any animals in the house.
h There are some books here — perhaps there are some ideas in them.

3 Put the words in the correct order.

1 help / any / Do / need / you ?
   Do you need any help?
2 information / like / some / about / I'd / concerts .
   ....
3 please / Can / some / some / eggs / and / I / have / cheese ?
   ....
4 yoghurt / there / in / Is / fridge / the / any ?
   ....
5 fun / out / have / and / Let's / some / go .
   ....
6 medicine / going / buy / for my cold / some / to / I'm .
   ....

4 Write the phrases in the correct places.

- any money
- some money
- any kids
- some kids
- ~~any examples~~
- some examples

1 I don't understand this very well — the teacher didn't give us ...*any examples*... .
2 It's free! You don't need .... to get in.
3 Sorry — you have to be over 18! We don't want .... in here.
4 It's a difficult bit of grammar. We need .... to help us.
5 There were .... at the shopping mall, but I didn't know them.
6 My parents gave me .... for my birthday, so I'm going to buy something nice.

5 Look at the picture. Write sentences.

1 cars — *There are some cars.*
2 bicycles — *There aren't*
3 kids — ....
4 dogs — ....
5 cats — ....
6 shops — ....

6 Complete the mini-dialogues with *some* or *any*.

1 A Have you got ......*any*...... CDs I can listen to?
   B Yes — I've got ......*some*...... CDs here in my backpack. Here you are.
2 A Mum — I've got .... problems with my homework.
   B Sorry dear — I haven't got .... time right now. Talk to me later.
3 A We need .... information about her for our project.
   B Well, I looked on the Internet but I didn't find .... information at all.
4 A The teacher didn't give us .... homework tonight.
   B Yes she did! She gave us .... grammar exercises to do.
5 A Let's go to the supermarket. We need to buy .... food.
   B OK, but don't forget we need .... money to buy things!

And now go to the CD-ROM and do the *Cartoon for Fun!*

Quantities

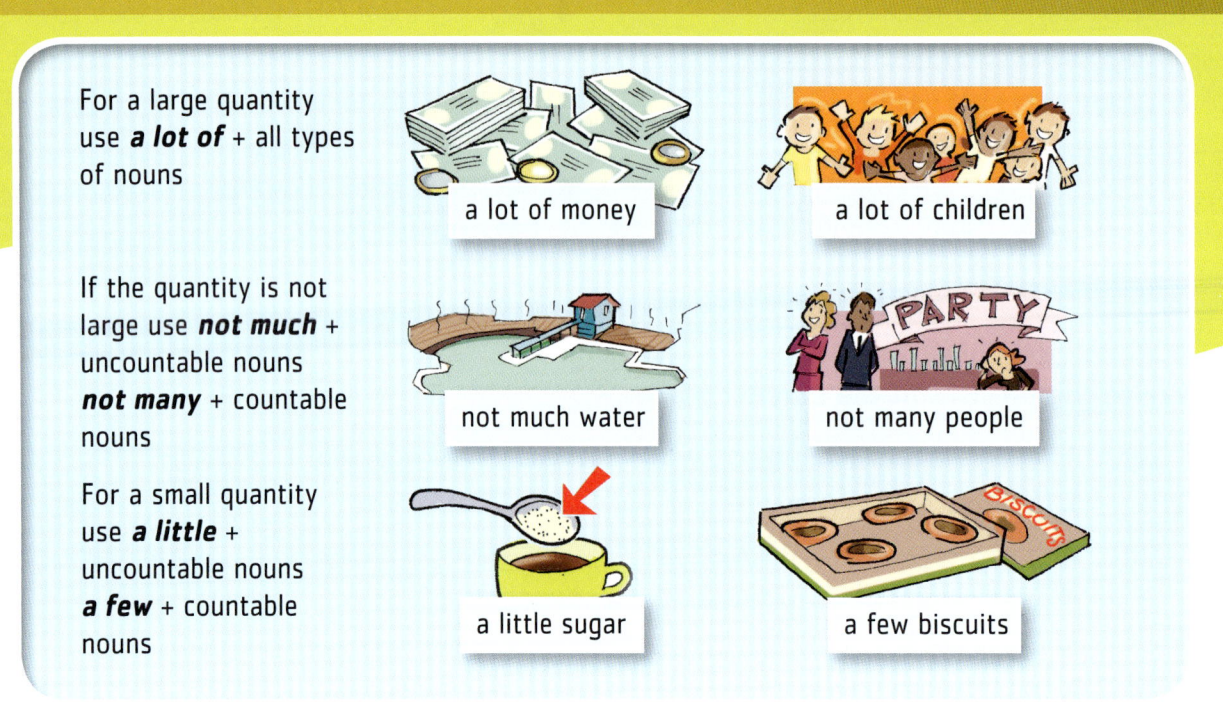

For a large quantity use **a lot of** + all types of nouns

a lot of money

a lot of children

If the quantity is not large use **not much** + uncountable nouns **not many** + countable nouns

not much water

not many people

For a small quantity use **a little** + uncountable nouns **a few** + countable nouns

a little sugar

a few biscuits

1 Choose the correct words to complete the story.

The Emperor's new clothes

An Emperor had ¹*a little / a lot of* elegant clothes but he wanted ²*some / any* more. Two tailors promised him a suit that only ³*a few / a little* people – the intelligent ones – could see. The Emperor believed them and ordered the suit. The two tailors asked for ⁴*a lot of / a little* money and pretended to work for ⁵*a few / a lot of* hours. They didn't use ⁶*much / many* material for the clothes, they didn't use ⁷*much / many* buttons or zips, but they took ⁸*any / a lot of* time to complete the suit. When it was ready, the Emperor went for a walk in the town and ⁹*a few / a lot of* people crowded the streets. Who could see the clothes? ¹⁰*Much / A lot of* people said they could see them but ¹¹*any / some* were in doubt. Then a little boy shouted 'The Emperor hasn't go ¹²*any / some* clothes on!' and everybody laughed except the naked Emperor.

2 Write the words in the correct order to write the recipe for a jam.

1 lot / raspberries / need / a / you / of
....

2 them / a lot / sugar / of / cover / with
....

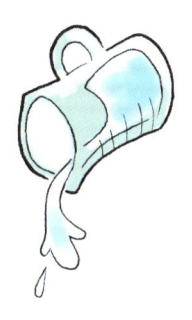

3 add / water / little / then / a
....

4 for / boil / few / hours / a / them
....

5 jam / pour / the / a / of / lot / jars / in
....

6 few / months / it / is / a / for / good
....

3 Complete the mini-dialogues with the 'quantity words' in the box.

lot (x2)
much
many
few (x2)
little (x2)

1 **A** How much milk have we got?
   B Just a ....

2 **A** How many biscuits are in the tin?
   B There are a .... The tin is full.

3 **A** How much coffee do you drink every day?
   B I don't drink .... , just one cup.

4 **A** Are there any tomatoes in the fridge?
   B I'm afraid there aren't .... , just two or three.

5 **A** Can I have some strawberries?
   B Oops, there are only a .... left.

6 **A** Do you want a lot of sugar?
   B No, I only want a ....

7 **A** Were there many people at your party?
   B Yes, there were a ....

8 **A** Why are you tired?
   B I only slept a .... hours last night.

Irregular plurals

With irregular plurals, always learn the singular and plural forms together.

one car – two car**s**

one child – two child**ren** (not two ~~childs~~)

1 Write the words under the pictures.

child
teeth
children
foot
tooth
people
feet
goose
person
~~geese~~
woman
women

1 ..geese.. 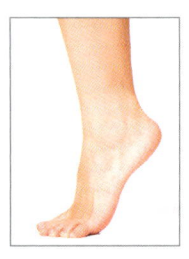 2  .... 3 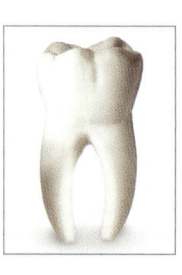 .... 4  .... 5  .... 6 ....

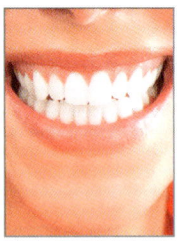

7  .... 8 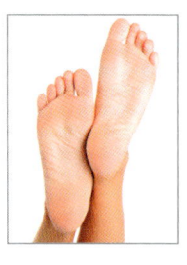 .... 9 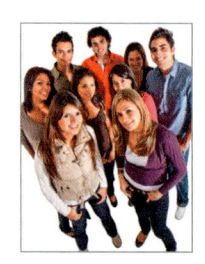 .... 10  .... 11  .... 12 ....

2 Write the plurals of the following words.

1 man   – ..men..................   3 thief – ....   5 fish – ....
2 knife – ....   4 leaf – ....   6 sheep – ....

3 Use words from **1** and **2** to complete the mini-dialogues.

1 A Did you have a good time fishing?
  B Yes, but I only caught two ..fish.. .
2 A I love autumn.
  B Me too. The .... on the trees are really beautiful colours.
3 A Why are you walking like that?
  B Because my right .... hurts.
4 A Is that a duck?
  B No, it's a ....

5 A Why are you going to the dentists?
  B Because my .... fell out. Look – here it is.
6 A Be careful with that .... It's very sharp.
  B Ow! Too late.
7 A How many .... do you want?
  B Two, a boy and a girl.
8 A Did the police catch the .... ?
  B They only caught one of them.

Questions with *who*

To ask a question about a person, use **who** + the verb in the 3rd person singular.

1 Match the questions with the picture answers.

1. Who plays Captain Jack Sparrow in *Pirates of the Caribbean*?
2. Who wrote *Romeo and Juliet*?
3. Who won the 2010 world cup?
4. Who is a comedy film star?
5. Who lives in Buckingham Palace?
6. Who became the President of the USA in 2008?

2 Write the questions for the answers.

1. **A** Who *told you* ?
   B Brian (told me).
2. **A** Who ....?
   B I don't know (who sent me the valentine card).
3. **A** Who ....?
   B Dad (paid for my new computer).
4. **A** Who ....?
   B I want to (watch another DVD).
5. **A** Who ....?
   B I'm not sure (who called the police).

3 Put the words in order to make questions.

1. Batman / Who / the / plays / new
   ....?
2. song / Who / this / sings
   ....?
3. wants / eat / to / now / Who
   ....?
4. that / you / lovely / gave / Who / jumper
   ....?
5. you / last / phoned / night / Who
   ....?

4 Match the questions in 3 with the answers.

1. My gran. It was a birthday present. ☐ 4
2. I'm not sure but it might be *U2*. ☐
3. Jo. She had a question about the homework. ☐
4. I do. I'm really hungry. ☐
5. Christian Bale. ☐

And now go to the CD-ROM and do the *Cartoon for Fun!*

Adverbs of manner

> Hello! See me on the CD-ROM to discover more about *adverbs of manner* and to learn better when to use them.

This is how you say how you do something.
Add **–ly** to the adjective.
Careful! **y** becomes **i + ly**.
There are also some exceptions that you need to learn!

Talk quiet**ly**.
She smiled happ**ily**.
He sings really **well**.

1 Find 10 adverbs and write them in the 2nd column in the table. (Look ↑ ↓ ← →.)

I	N	T	E	L	L	I	G	E	N	T	L	Y	K
E	U	A	A	Q	S	K	H	F	U	G	K	L	N
G	J	E	S	E	P	O	F	H	G	F	A	S	T
N	E	R	I	T	E	E	J	B	F	K	L	U	B
J	H	F	L	H	N	A	Z	N	S	V	M	O	S
Y	G	D	Y	J	K	N	Y	E	E	W	G	R	R
L	M	Y	L	T	H	G	I	R	B	Y	N	E	E
S	P	O	C	H	B	R	R	V	D	L	C	G	N
U	Y	S	Q	U	T	I	E	O	G	R	Y	N	B
O	T	F	D	M	Y	L	L	U	F	E	R	A	C
I	B	S	R	M	S	Y	K	S	R	V	Q	D	H
R	U	T	Z	P	A	L	U	L	O	E	I	S	T
U	W	N	O	Z	U	G	H	Y	T	L	K	L	P
F	K	P	L	Y	K	L	U	Z	D	C	D	J	R

adjective	adverb
intelligent	intelligently

2 Write the adjectives and complete the first column in the table in **1**.

3 Write the adverbs for the adjectives.

angry — *angrily*   boring — ....   good — ....   excited — ....
bad — ....   happy — ....   fast — ....   easy — ....
clever — ....   tired — ....   serious — ....   terrible — ....

4 Find the opposites.

~~jokingly~~   badly   well
slowly   terribly   quietly
brilliantly   happily   quickly
loudly   sadly   ~~seriously~~

jokingly — seriously   .... — ....
.... — .... — ....
.... — .... — ....

5 Underline the correct adverb.

1 I did really *badly / dangerously / cleverly* in the test. I got 25%!
2 He shouted at us *boringly / jokingly / furiously*. He wasn't happy at all!
3 He passed his driving test *intelligently / easily / fast*. He had no problems.
4 The stars shone *quietly / slowly / brightly* in the sky.
5 'I've won the lottery!' he told us *cleverly / sadly / excitedly*.
6 He speaks Italian *dangerously / nervously / brilliantly*. He's like an Italian.
7 He ran really *slowly / furiously / fast* and won the race.
8 He did his homework *boringly / carefully / jokingly* and made no mistakes.

6 Look at the underlined word. Write adverb or adjective.

1 We walked slowly to school. — *adverb*
2 It was a beautiful Monday morning. — ....
3 Don't get close to that dog. It's dangerous. — ....
4 The dog barked at us furiously. — ....
5 She speaks French very well. — ....
6 She always gets good grades in her French tests. — ....
7 That was a difficult question. — ....
8 I think he answered that question very intelligently. — ....

7 Complete the sentences with the adverbs in the box.

angrily
dangerously
loudly
happily
carefully
~~brightly~~
quietly
furiously

1 It's a normal Monday morning. The sun is shining *brightly*.
2 Inside the classroom, Mr Lame is talking ....
3 Nobody is listening. Dan is whispering .... into May's ear.
4 Kevin is smiling .... at Betty.
5 Betty is looking .... at Kevin.
6 Only Emily is listening .... She's Mr Lame's favourite.
7 Steve is sitting on his chair ....
8 Now Mr Lame is shouting .... Yes, it's a normal Monday morning.

8 How do these people speak? Follow the lines to find out and then write sentences.

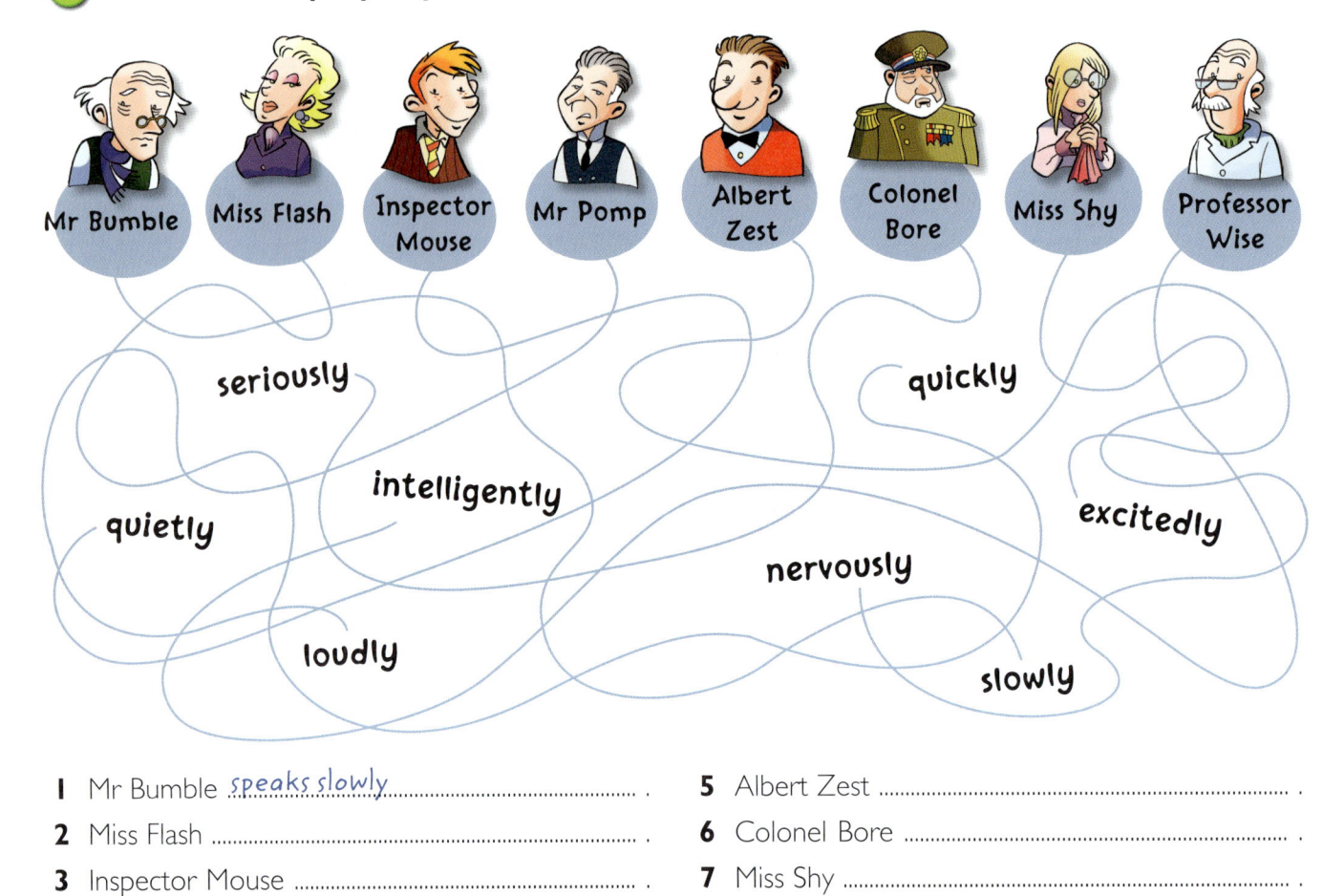

Mr Bumble · Miss Flash · Inspector Mouse · Mr Pomp · Albert Zest · Colonel Bore · Miss Shy · Professor Wise

seriously · quickly · intelligently · quietly · excitedly · nervously · loudly · slowly

1 Mr Bumble *speaks slowly* .
2 Miss Flash ....
3 Inspector Mouse ....
4 Mr Pomp ....
5 Albert Zest ....
6 Colonel Bore ....
7 Miss Shy ....
8 Professor Wise ....

9 Read the beginning of the story and underline the correct words.

Mr Bumble was a ¹ *rich / richly* man but not anymore because Mr Bumble was dead. Mr Bumble had nothing now but a ² *sharp / sharply* knife in his back. Inspector Mouse looked ³ *careful / carefully* at the body. Then he turned around ⁴ *quick / quickly* and spoke ⁵ *excited / excitedly* to his friend Albert Zest. This was unusual because Inspector Mouse usually spoke ⁶ *quiet / quietly* but at this moment he was very ⁷ *excited / excitedly*.

'This knife did not kill Mr Bumble.' He said. 'Look at these ⁸ *bright / brightly* spots around his mouth. Cyanide killed him!'

'But who gave him the poison?' asked Zest.

'That is what I need to find out ⁹ *loud / loudly*.' Replied the Inspector 'And I am going to need your help young man. There were five people in the house yesterday afternoon at the time of the murder. They were all there to celebrate Mr Bumble's 80th birthday tomorrow. We need to talk ¹⁰ *serious / seriously* with all of them.'

10 Read the next part of the story and complete with the adverbs of the adjectives.

Inspector Mouse looked ¹...carefully... (careful) at his notes and told Albert Zest about the suspects.

"Colonel Bore is an old army friend of Mr Bumble. He reacted ²................... (bad) when I told him about the murder. He was very sad. He also has a good alibi because he wasn't at the house all afternoon. He was in the village visiting an aunt. And there are lots of witnesses who saw him driving his Rolls Royce ³................... (slow) along the roads."

"I didn't like Mr Pomp. He spoke ⁴................... (rude) to me and didn't want to help at all. He's Mr Bumble's secretary. He organised the weekend and invited everyone to the party. When I asked him why he wanted Mr Bumble dead he reacted ⁵................... (angry) and told me he hasn't got a job any more."

"Miss Shy is an interesting woman. She met Mr Bumble on the Internet. They both enjoy bird-watching and spent weekends away together. When I asked her about romance she reacted ⁶................... (furious). I don't think she liked my question."

Professor Wise is a chemistry professor at London university. He's very well-educated and can talk ⁷................... (intelligent) about anything. He's an old school friend of Mr Bumble. He says he saw Colonel Bore shouting ⁸................... (loud) with Mr Bumble about half an hour before the murder.

"Miss Flash spoke ⁹................... (nervous) when I asked her questions. But she's a nervous person so maybe that's not a very important fact. She knew Mr Bumble ¹⁰................... (good) because she worked for him for forty years."

So Zest. What do you think? Do you know who our murderer is?

11 Who do you think the murderer is? Read the solution at the bottom of the page.

12 Rewrite the sentences to include the words.

1 He did his homework but he still made a mistake. (carefully / big)
   He did his homework carefully but he still made a big mistake.

2 It was a Maths test and I finished. (easy / quickly)

3 I walked because I had a bag. (slowly / heavy)

4 It was a summer day and the sun shone. (lovely / brightly)

5 I had to talk because it was a party. (loudly / noisy)

6 The children got up and opened their presents. (early / excitedly)

7 My dad drove and we were all passengers. (dangerously / nervous)

8 It was a song and she sang it. (brilliant / well)

13 Answer the questions about you.

How do you:

1 talk?
   I talk quickly.

2 walk?

3 do your homework?

4 speak English?

5 dance?

6 open birthday presents?

7 cook?

8 play tennis?

Professor Wise is the murderer. He says he saw Colonel Bore shouting with Mr Bumble just before the murder. Bore has an alibi for the afternoon so Wise is lying. Also because he is a Chemistry professor he can easily get hold of cyanide.

And now go to the CD-ROM and do the *Cartoon for Fun!*

whose + possessive 's

This is how you can ask and talk about who something belongs to.

Whose is this bag?   It's Kevin**'s** (bag).
It's Doris' (bag).

1 Write the answers to the questions. Use the names in the box to help you.

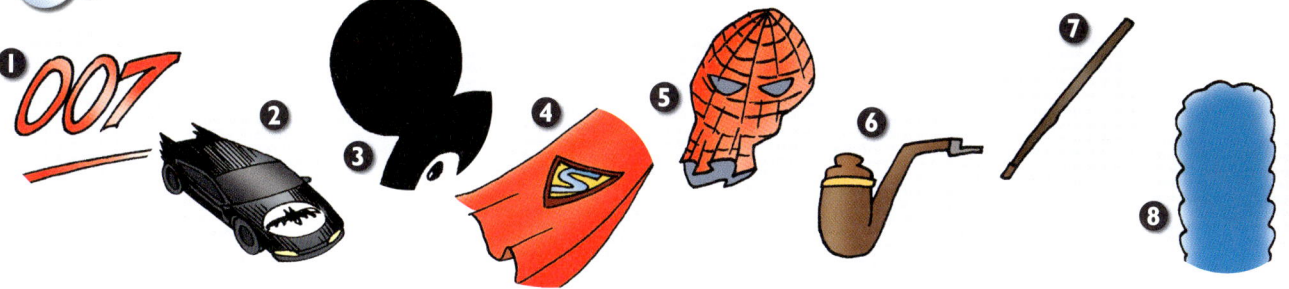

Spiderman
Harry Potter
Mickey Mouse
Superman
Batman
~~James Bond~~
Marge Simpson
Sherlock Holmes

1 Whose is this codename?
   It's James Bond's codename.
2 Whose is this car?
   ....
3 Whose is this ear?
   ....
4 Whose is this cape?
   ....
5 Whose is this mask?
   ....
6 Whose is this pipe?
   ....
7 Whose is this wand?
   ....
8 Whose is this hair?
   ....

2 Look at the picture and write dialogues about the objects.

1 A Whose are these earrings?
   B They're Kerry's earrings.

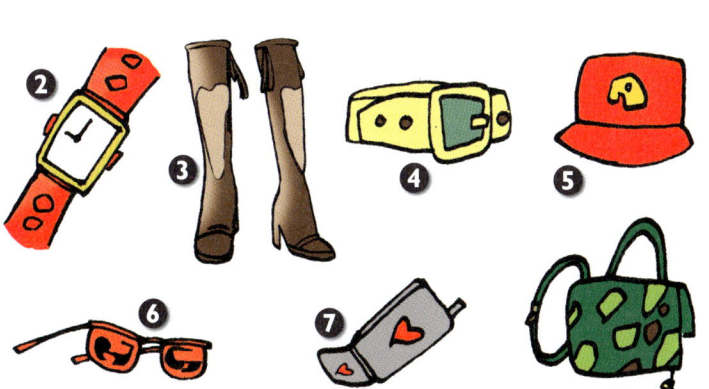

And now go to the CD-ROM and do the **Cartoon for Fun!**

Possessive pronouns

This is how you can say that something belongs to you or to another person.

1 Complete the table with the words in the box.

ours, hers, ~~his~~, his, theirs, yours, your, ~~my~~, their, our, mine, her

I	That's ....*my*.... bike.	That's ....
You	That's .... bike.	That's ....
He	That's .... bike.	That's ....*his*.......... .
She	That's .... bike.	That's ....
We	That's .... bike.	That's ....
They	That's .... bike.	That's ....

2 Choose the correct option.

1 Don't worry. It's not *your* / yours problem.
2 It not your problem. It's her / hers.
3 Excuse me. That pizza. I think it's our / ours.
4 Don't eat it. It's their / theirs.
5 This is where we live. This is our / ours home.
6 Their / Theirs dog is really ugly.
7 These are my shoes and those are your / yours.
8 I really like her / hers trousers.

3 Follow the lines. Complete the sentences with the correct possessive pronoun.

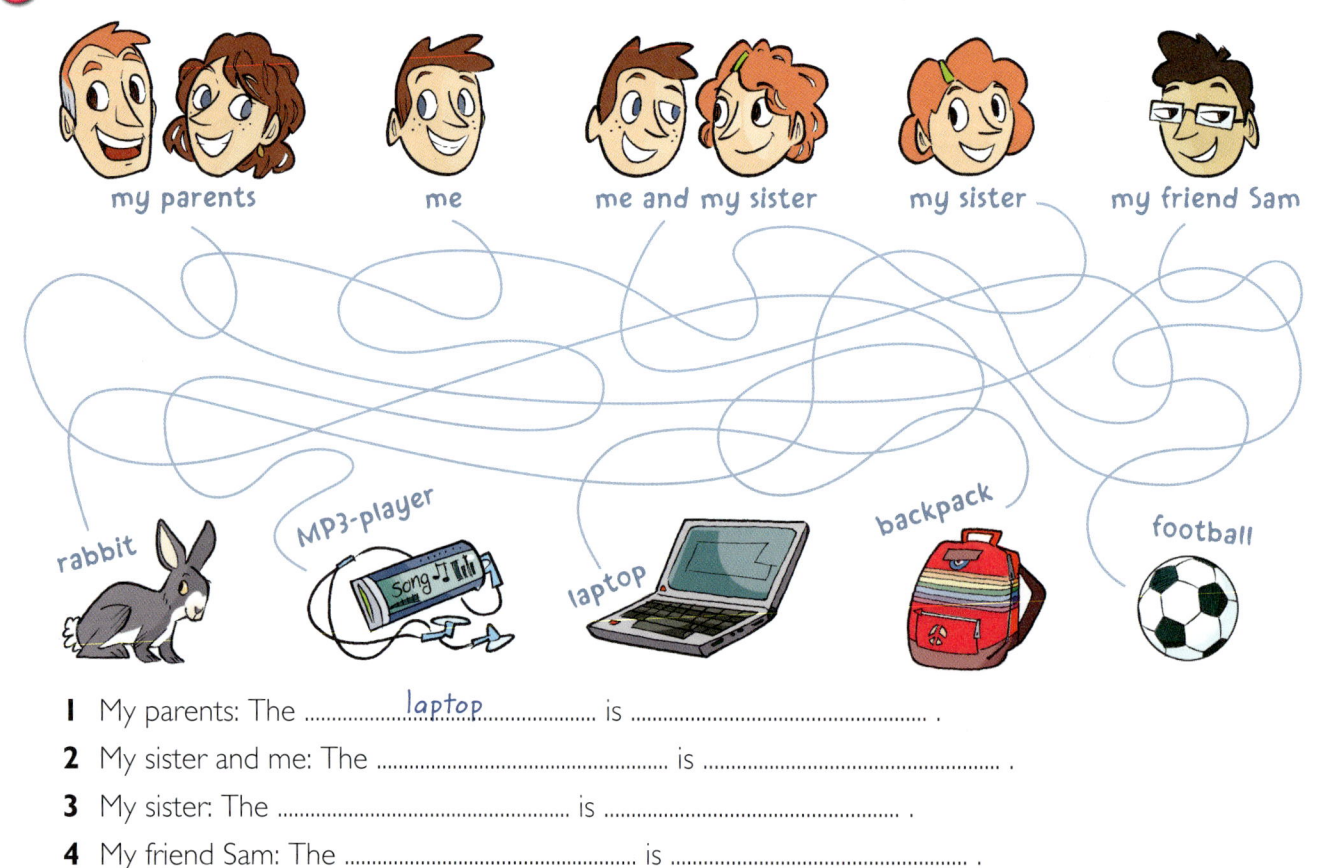

my parents — me — me and my sister — my sister — my friend Sam

rabbit — MP3-player — laptop — backpack — football

1 My parents: The ......*laptop*...... is ....
2 My sister and me: The .... is ....
3 My sister: The .... is ....
4 My friend Sam: The .... is ....
5 Me: The .... is ....

4 Complete the sentences with the missing pronouns.

1. It's not my ball. It's *theirs*.
2. I'm sorry but I don't think it's ....
3. If anyone gives you a lion, it's probably ....
4. Excuse me. I think that cake is ....
5. I think it's ....
6. No, it's not my dog. I think it's ....

5 Complete the dialogues with the missing words.

Teacher Hi Mike, someone left this scarf in the classroom. Is it ¹*yours*?

Mike No it's not ²............... scarf. Ask Bill. I think it's ³............... .

(Two minutes later.)

Teacher Bill, is this ⁴............... scarf?

Bill Let me have a look. No, it's not ⁵............... . It might be Jane's scarf. Ask ⁶............... .

(Two minutes later.)

Teacher Jane? Is this ⁷...............?

Jane No, it's the twins'.

Teacher Richard and Henry? Is it ⁸............... scarf?

Jane Yes, I think it's ⁹............... .

(Two minutes later.)

Teacher Richard, Henry. Is this ¹⁰...............?

Twins No, it's not ¹¹............... .

Teacher ¹²............... scarf is it?

Henry Can I have a look at it?

Teacher Sure. Here you are.

Henry It's got the initials KL. Aren't those ¹³............... initials, sir?

Teacher Yes, they're ¹⁴............... initials.

Henry I think this is ¹⁵............... scarf, sir.

Teacher Oh yes. It is. It's ¹⁶............... .

And now go to the CD-ROM and do the *Cartoon for Fun!*

Past participles

You use the *past participle* (or *third form*) of a verb to form the *present perfect*. There are regular and irregular forms. For regular verbs, add **–ed** or **–d** to the base form.

Regular			Irregular		
Infinitive	Past Simple	Past Participle	Infinitive	Past Simple	Past Participle
pass	pass**ed**	pass**ed**	go	went	**gone**
walk	walk**ed**	walk**ed**	see	saw	**seen**
move	mov**ed**	mov**ed**	come	came	**come**
talk	talk**ed**	talk**ed**	cut	cut	**cut**

1 Find twelve past participles in the wordsnake.

Seen gone bought fallen cut been won broken lost had come taken

2 Write the words from **1** in the correct places to complete the table.

1	go	went	gone
2	see	saw	
3	come	came	
4	cut	cut	
5	be	was/were	
6	take	took	

7	win	won	
8	break	broke	
9	buy	bought	
10	fall	fell	
11	lose	lost	
12	have	had	

3 Use a word from **1** to complete each sentence.

1 Look! Inspector Groans has ......*fallen*...... out of a tree again!
2 I'm not hungry, thanks – I've .... lunch.
3 John's not here – he's .... into town to do some shopping.
4 Look – I've .... three new CDs. Do you want to listen to them?
5 I'm really happy because my team has .... the championship!
6 There's blood on my finger – I think I've .... it.
7 We've only been here two days, and my sister has .... 100 photographs already!
8 Do you know where my book is? I've .... it!

Present perfect

> Hello! See me on the CD-ROM to discover more about the *present perfect* and to learn better when to use it.

You use the *present perfect* to say that something has happened in the recent past, or just now. Don't use fixed past time expressions with the *present perfect*.

✓ I / You / We / They **'ve bought** (=**have bought**) a new pair of shoes.
He / She / It **'s been** (=**has been**) here a long time.

✗ I / You / We / They **haven't** (=**have not**) **bought** a new pair of shoes.
He / She / It **hasn't** (=**has not**) **been** here a long time.

? **Have** I / you / we / they **eaten** too much?
Has he / she / it **been** here a long time?

1 Write the sentences using short forms.

1 We have not been here before.
   We haven't been here before.
2 It has not rained for a long time.
   ....
3 I have bought a new book.
   ....
4 My parents have not seen this film.
   ....
5 He has always worked here.
   ....
6 We have not eaten our lunch.
   ....
7 You have listened to all my CDs.
   ....
8 My favourite band has made a new CD.
   ....

2 Match the pictures and the sentences.

1 I've won!
2 He's lost his glasses.
3 They haven't had their dinner.
4 We've been to the shops.
5 I think I've broken my leg.
6 I've seen it – it's really good.
7 He's fallen off his bike.
8 She's swum 3 kilometres.

3 Make the sentences negative.

1 I've bought a new laptop.   *I haven't bought a new laptop.*
2 We've moved house.   ....
3 They've come back from their holiday. ....
4 I've studied for tomorrow's test. ....
5 My dad's made dinner.   ....

4 Match the sentences to make mini-dialogues.

1 Where are your glasses?
2 Is Jenny here?
3 Would you like some more?
4 Why does she know so much about Italy?
5 Is your dog ill?'
6 Your mum speaks good French, doesn't she?
7 Is High School Musical your favourite film?
8 Why don't you phone him?
9 Someone told me that your mother's a writer.
10 You look very happy.
11 I phoned you last night — no answer.
12 Why isn't Tom here?

a She's been there about ten times!
b Yes. I think it's eaten something bad.
c I can't — I've lost his number.
d Yes. She's written about six books.
e I don't know. I've lost them.
f He's gone to Italy on holiday.
g No, she's gone to see her friend Amy.
h I am. I've had some good news!
i Yes, she does. She's lived in Paris.
j Yeah, sorry — I've lost my mobile phone.
k No, I've eaten lots, thank you.
l Yes, I've seen it about ten times!

5 Read the dialogue. Put the verbs into the correct form of the present perfect.

A You look tired.
B I am. I ¹ 've been .... (be) very busy.
A Oh? What ² .... you .... (do)?
B Well, I ³ .... (tidy) my room.
A Good — it was terrible before! And …?
B And I ⁴ .... (do) my homework.
A Excellent. ⁵ .... you .... (feed) the hamster?
B No — the hamster isn't hungry. But I ⁶ .... (clean) its cage.
A Well, you're right — you ⁷ .... (be) busy! Just one more question.
B Yes?
A ⁸ .... you .... (cook) dinner for us?
B Mum — give me a break!

6 Put the words in order to make sentences and questions.

1 gone / America / My / to / has / dad
   My dad has gone to America.
2 me / hasn't / phoned / Timothy
   ....
3 windsurfing / I've / three times / been
   ....
4 countries / I've / to / different / travelled / of / lots
   ....
5 this / times / read / book / I've / four
   ....
6 all / eaten / chocolate / has / Tess / the
   ....
7 their / Have / CD / new / you / heard / ?
   ....
8 homework / the / Has / us / given / any / teacher / ?
   ....

60

7 Complete with the words in the box.

climbed
found
learned
made
swum
~~travelled~~
taken
walked
written

In my life ...
I've ¹ *travelled* round the world.
I've ² .... lots of mountains.
I've ³ .... in lakes and rivers.
I've ⁴ .... across deserts.
I've ⁵ .... thousands of photographs.
I've ⁶ .... lots of new friends.
I've ⁷ .... twenty languages.
I've ⁸ .... a hundred poems.
But ... I haven't ⁹ .... a man to love!

8 Complete the sentences. Use the present perfect form of the verbs in the box.

eat
not learn
not open
see
travel
~~play~~
work
win
not write
not listen

1 I'm bored with this game now – I *'ve played* it hundreds of times!
2 I've got some new CDs, but I .... to them.
3 I .... Indian food lots of times.
4 Uncle James sent me a birthday present – but I .... it yet.
5 It's a nice film, but I .... much better ones.
6 My aunt Jessica .... to more than fifteen different countries!
7 He's my favourite tennis player – he .... Wimbledon six times!
8 I love cars, but I .... how to drive.
9 My dad .... for more than ten different companies.
10 I wrote an email to my friend, but she .... back to me.

9 Put the verbs into the present perfect.

One of my friends at school is Dilap. His parents are from India – they came to Britain twenty-five years ago. They live in the same street as me – they ¹ *'ve* always *lived* (live) in the same house. Dilap and I went to the same junior school and we ² .... (be) friends since then.

Dilap's really smart. He plays chess and he's very good – he ³ .... (win) lots of school tournaments. He ⁴ .... (beat) the chess teacher lots of times, too! He's also really good at Maths and at Information Technology. Dilap says that people from India ⁵ .... always .... (be) good with computers and things like that. He ⁶ .... (try) to teach me things about IT, but he ⁷ .... never .... (be) very successful!

Dilap ⁸ .... (visit) India about six times, I think – his family goes back every year to see their relatives. He ⁹ .... always .... (enjoy) the visits to India, he says. I'd love to go with him one day – but so far, he ¹⁰ .... (not invite) me!

And now go to the CD-ROM and do the **Cartoon for Fun!**

Present perfect + already / yet

We often use the *present perfect* with the word **already**. We also often use it with **not yet**.

I **'ve already** washed the car.
We **'ve already** seen this film.
I **haven't done** my homework **yet**.
She **hasn't told** him **yet**.

1 Match the pictures with sentences.

1. He's already had a shower.
2. He hasn't had a shower yet.
3. We've already eaten.
4. We haven't eaten yet.
5. He hasn't caught a fish yet.
6. He's already caught two fish.
7. He hasn't fed the dog yet.
8. He's already fed the dog.

2 Complete the newspaper article with the phrases in the box.

already competed
US yet
already attracted
already broken
18 yet
~~already won~~
already earned
gold medal yet

Welcome to Nathan Holmes
Britain's newest star in the swimming pool

He's ¹ *already won* the 100 m and 200 m freestyle British championship. And he's ² .... the UK record at both these distances. And he's not even turned ³ .... He only does that in November.
He's ⁴ .... all over Europe but he hasn't swum in the ⁵ .... Next year he starts training in LA. It's a dream come true.

He's ⁶ .... more than £100,000 in prize money. And the really big money is going to come soon because he's ⁷ .... the interest of some very important companies.
And his biggest dream of all – the Olympics. He hasn't won an Olympic ⁸ .... But we're sure he's going to win one soon.

3 Write the sentences using short forms.

1 I have not seen this film yet.
   I haven't seen this film yet.
2 She has not spoken to me yet.
   ....
3 Henry has already written the email.
   ....
4 I have already asked my mum.
   ....
5 My dad has already found a new job.
   ....
6 They have not invited me to their party yet.
   ....
7 You have already told me that.
   ....
8 We have not finished our lunch yet.
   ....

4 Complete the sentences with the present perfect forms of the verbs.

1 She **'s** already **bought** a new dress but no one **'s** **invited** her to the party yet. (buy / invite)
2 He .... to play the guitar yet but he .... already .... an expensive guitar. (not learn / get)
3 She .... already .... the washing-up but we .... dinner yet. (do / not finish)
4 I .... you the question yet but you .... already .... me your answer. (not ask / give)
5 I .... that film yet but he .... already .... me the end of it. (not see / tell)
6 You .... already .... off your coat but the rain .... yet. (take / not stop)
7 She .... already .... on the lights but it .... dark yet. (turn / not get)
8 He .... his computer yet and he .... already .... it. (not use / break)

5 Complete the dialogue with yet or already.

Tim Come on Paul, let's go.
Paul I'm not ready ¹ *yet* .
Tim What! But the film starts in half an hour.
Paul That's OK. I've ² .... ordered a taxi for 7.30.
Tim 7.30! The film starts at 7.45!
Paul So what's the problem?
Tim The problem is that we haven't got our tickets ³ ....
Paul Yes we have.
Tim We have?
Paul I've ⁴ .... told you twice.
Tim So tell me again.
Paul I've ⁵ .... bought our tickets. I got them online.
Tim Online?
Paul Look, here they are. Two tickets for *The Final Conflict*.
Tim *The Final Conflict*! But I've ⁶ .... seen *The Final Conflict*!
Paul Whoops!

6 **Write the questions and then match them with the answers below.**

1 you / phone / Carl
   Have you phoned Carl yet? — e

2 you / play / Kingdom of Doom
   ....?

3 you / sell / your computer
   ....?

4 you / fix / your bike
   ....?

5 she / invite / you to her party
   ....?

6 she / give / you a birthday present
   ....?

7 he / do / the washing-up
   ....?

8 he / finish / the book
   ....?

a Yes, he did it straight after dinner.
b No, it's still broken.
c No, I think she's forgotten.
d I think he's on the last chapter.
e I tried but he didn't answer.
f No. No one wants to buy it.
g I got to level 2 and I gave up.
h Yes, she gave me an invitation yesterday.

7 **Look at John's list and write sentences about what he has already done and what he hasn't done yet.**

1 *He's already washed the car.*
2 ....
3 ....
4 ....
5 ....
6 ....
7 ....
8 ....

8 Look at the picture and then decide if the sentences are True or False.

1 The red team have already scored four goals. ....True....
2 The first half hasn't finished yet. ....
3 The blue team haven't scored a goal yet. ....
4 The red number four has just got a red card. ....
5 The second half has already started. ....
6 The blue number ten hasn't taken the penalty yet. ....
7 It hasn't started raining yet. ....
8 A fan has just run onto the pitch. ....

9 Rewrite the sentences and include the word.

1 I've seen Janice. (just)
   I've just seen Janice.
2 He's told me your secret. (already)
   ....
3 We haven't had lunch. (yet)
   ....
4 Paula's gone to the shops. (just)
   ....
5 The dog's had its puppies. (already)
   ....
6 Don hasn't bought a new car. (yet)
   ....
7 Mum's broken a cup. (just)
   ....
8 I haven't send him the email. (yet)
   ....

10 Complete the postcard using the present perfect form of the verbs.

Hi Paula,
Week three of our European tour already. Time goes too fast. We ¹ *'ve already spent* (already spend) time in France and Spain and now we're in the UK. I'm in London! Can you believe it? We've only been here two days but we ² .... (already have) a wonderful time. We've done so many things. We ³ .... (already be) on the London Eye — fantastic and we ⁴ .... (already see) Buckingham Palace but I ⁵ .... the Queen .... (not meet yet). Tomorrow we're going to do some more sightseeing: the Tower of London, Hyde Park and Covent Garden. We ⁶ .... a show .... (not see yet) but mum ⁷ .... (already promise) to take us to one tonight.
We've been so busy that we ⁸ .... any shopping .... (not do yet) so I ⁹ .... you a present .... (not buy yet).
So far we've walked everywhere. We ¹⁰ .... on the Underground .... (not travel yet). London is so big. We ¹¹ .... (already get) lost lots of times. But that's always fun. You find new exciting places.
More soon. Bye!

11 **Put the words in order to make sentences.**

1 shopping / We / yet / done / the / haven't
   We haven't done the shopping yet.

2 bought / just / a / TV / We've / new

3 woken / yet / hasn't / She / up

4 sandwiches / You / two / already / had / have

5 games / They've / finished / just / computer / playing

6 baby / My / just / mum's / new / had / a

7 yet / I / Batman / seen / the / haven't / new / film

8 walk / I've / a / the / dog / taken / already / for

12 **Make the positive sentences negative and the negative sentences positive.**

1 I haven't tidied my room yet.
   I've already tidied my room.

2 Oliver's already given me a present.

3 She hasn't phoned her mum yet.

4 Mum and Dad have already gone out.

5 I've already done my exams.

6 They haven't had dinner yet.

7 Sally's already sold her skateboard.

8 We haven't found our dog yet.

13 **Use the word prompts to write about yourself.**

take / driving test — *I haven't taken my driving test yet. I'm too young!*
decide / future job
fall off / bike
fly / airplane
go / abroad
break / leg
learn / swim
have / boy/girlfriend — *That's none of your business!*

And now go to the CD-ROM and do the **Cartoon for Fun!**

Present perfect + ever / never

You use the *present perfect* with **ever / never** to ask about things someone has done or not done in their life up to now.

Have you **ever** been to Hollywood?

Has she **ever** met a famous person?

I've **never** been to Hollywood.

She's **never** met a famous person.

1 Complete the poem with the words in the box.

Have
phone
eaten
holidays
foreign
stay
ever
never
found
Paris
please
done

Too many questions

Have you ever ¹.................. foreign food?
Have you ².................. broken a bone?
Have you ever been to ³..................?
⁴.................. you ever been to Rome?

No I've never eaten ⁵.................. food.
And I've ⁶.................. broken a bone.
And I never go on ⁷.................. .
I prefer to ⁸.................. at home.

Have you ever ⁹.................. a wallet?
Have you ever lost your ¹⁰..................?
No, I've never ¹¹.................. those things.
Now ¹² .... leave me alone.

2 Match questions and answers.

1 Have you ever been to a fancy dress party?
2 Have you ever had an accident?
3 Have you ever done a parachute jump?
4 Have you ever seen a ghost?
5 Have you ever broken your leg?
6 Have you ever got stuck in a lift?
7 Have you ever deleted an important computer file by mistake?
8 Have you ever written a short story.

a I've never seen one because they don't exist.
b Yes, I wore an Egyptian mummy costume.
c Yes, it was my dad's and he was furious with me.
d No, I haven't. I'm not very creative.
e No, I've never done one and I don't ever want to do one.
f No. I've never broken anything.
g I fell off my bike once but it wasn't very serious.
h Yes, I got stuck in one for half an hour. It was quite scared.

3 Put the words in order to make sentences or questions.

1 had / ever / you / dog / a / Have   ....
2 accident / had / She's / an / never   ....
3 been / never / They've / on / airplane / an   ....
4 famous / she / person / ever / met / a / Has   ....
5 dress / We've / fancy / been / to / never / a / party   ....

4 Read the radio interview and complete it with the phrases in the box.

- have you ever thought
- have you ever broken
- 've fallen into
- haven't broken
- 've been on TV
- 've broken
- 've written
- 've fallen out
- 've fallen off
- 've had
- 've crashed
- 've never thought
- 've met some famous people
- 've never broken

DJ In the studio today we have Arnold Bump. Arnold is the world's unluckiest man.
Arnold That's right. I hold the world record for the unluckiest man on Earth.
DJ So Arnold, how did you get that record?
Arnold It's quite simple. I ¹.................................. a lot of accidents.
DJ Can you tell us about some?
Arnold Certainly. I ².................................. the River Thames in London. I ³.................................. of a 20 m tree. I ⁴.................................. my bike about 20 times and I ⁵.................................. my car five times.
DJ Wow. And ⁶.................................. any bones?
Arnold I ⁷.................................. lots of bones. I think the only bone I ⁸.................................. is my left arm. No, I ⁹.................................. that one.
DJ It sounds terrible.
Arnold Well it's not all bad. I ¹⁰.................................. and I ¹¹.................................. and I ¹².................................. a book about it all.
DJ And ¹³.................................. about making a film about your life?
Arnold No, I ¹⁴.................................. about that but it's not a bad idea.

5 Write the questions.

1 _Have you ever fallen out of a tree_? (fall)
2 ....? (fall asleep)
3 ....? (be on TV)
4 ....? (win)
5 ....? (eat)
6 ....? (be)
7 ....? (travel by)
8 ....? (drive)

6 Write your answers to the questions in **5**.

And now go to the CD-ROM and do the *Cartoon for Fun!*

So (do/have) I / Neither (do/have) I

> Hello! See me on the CD-ROM to discover more about *So (do/have) I / Neither (do/have) I* and to learn better when to use them.

Sometimes you want to say something like 'The same thing is true for me'. You can do this using the words **So** or **Neither** with the verb in question word order. With modal verbs (**can / can't, must / mustn't** etc) and **have**, you don't use **do / did**.

I like rap – **So do** I.
I've got a laptop. – **So have** I.
I can play the piano. – **So can** I.
I went to the cinema last night. – **So did** I.

I don't like rock. – **Neither do** I.
I haven't got a laptop – **Neither have** I.
I can't play the piano. – **Neither can** I.
I didn't go to the cinema last night. – **Neither did** I.

1 Underline the correct answers.

1. **A** I want an ice cream.
   B <u>So do I</u> / Neither do I.
2. **A** I live in Grange Road.
   B *So do I / So have I.*
3. **A** I've got a test tomorrow.
   B *So do I / So have I.*
4. **A** I've got a new bike.
   B *So have I / Neither have I.*
5. **A** I don't like her.
   B *So do I / Neither do I.*
6. **A** I don't eat meat.
   B *Neither do I / Neither have I.*
7. **A** I haven't got any money.
   B *So have I / Neither have I.*
8. **A** I haven't done my homework yet.
   B *Neither do I / Neither have I.*

2 Complete the dialogues with the sentences in the box.

So do I. (2x)
Neither do I. (2x)
So have I. (2x)
~~Neither have I. (2x)~~

1. **A** I haven't got a pet.
   B *Neither have I.*
2. **A** I really like Brad Pitt.
   B ....
3. **A** I've got a headache.
   B ....
4. **A** I don't play tennis very well.
   B ....
5. **A** I haven't seen this film.
   B ....
6. **A** I don't get up early at the weekend.
   B ....
7. **A** I've finished my homework.
   B ....
8. **A** I go swimming three times a week.
   B ....

3 Match the sentences and replies.

1. I collect postcards.
2. I don't walk to school.
3. I've lost my school bag.
4. I've not watched TV all day.
5. I can speak three languages.
6. I can't go to Dave's party.
7. I went to bed late last night.
8. I didn't enjoy the book.

a. So have I.
b. So can I.
c. Neither can I.
d. So did I.
e. So do I.
f. Neither have I.
g. Neither did I.
h. Neither do I.

4 Fill in the blanks and complete the dialogue. Choose from So do/have I, Neither do/have I.

Lucy I love Beyoncé.
Emma ¹ *So do I.* . She's brilliant.
Lucy I've got all her CDs.
Emma ² .... All of them.
Lucy Actually I haven't got her first one.
Emma No, ³............................. .
Lucy But I want to get it.
Emma ⁴............................. . I'm going to get it tomorrow.
Lucy I don't think she's done a bad song.
Emma ⁵............................. . They're all great.
Lucy I also think she's a great actress.
Emma ⁶............................. . She's really great.
Lucy I've seen all her films.
Emma ⁷............................. . I love them.
Lucy I've never seen her in a bad film.
Emma ⁸............................. . She's always brilliant.
Lucy Actually I'm just joking. I think she's terrible really.
Emma Yeah ⁹............................. . She's rubbish.

5 Complete with so or neither.

1 **A** I only wear black clothes.
   B ...*So*... do I.
2 **A** I can't stand on my head.
   B .... can I.
3 **A** I bought a new T-shirt yesterday.
   B .... did I.
4 **A** I don't want to go home yet.
   B .... do I.
5 **A** I didn't watch all the film.
   B .... did I.
6 **A** I haven't read this book yet.
   B .... have I.
7 **A** I can't do this homework.
   B .... can I.
8 **A** I've got a cold.
   B .... have I.

6 Write the replies.

1 **A** I haven't been to London.
   B *Neither have I.*
2 **A** I didn't go to school yesterday.
   B ....
3 **A** I can't play tennis very well.
   B ....
4 **A** I never read the newspaper.
   B ....
5 **A** I saw a great film last night.
   B ....
6 **A** I always have a drink of milk before I go to sleep.
   B ....
7 **A** I've got two cats.
   B ....
8 **A** I can see a problem with this.
   B ....

And now go to the CD-ROM and do the **Cartoon for Fun!**

Appendix

TENSES

PRESENT TENSE

Present simple

We form the *Present simple* with the base form of the verb.
We add **-s** to the base form for the third person singular (**he** / **she** / **it**).

Affirmative	Negative	Questions	Short answers	
I **like** London.	I **don't (do not) like** London.	**Do/Don't** I **like** London?	Yes, I **do**.	No, I **don't**.
You **like** London.	You **don't (do not) like** London.	**Do/Don't** you **like** London?	Yes, you **do**.	No, you **don't**.
He **likes** London.	He **doesn't (does not) like** London.	**Does/Doesn't** he **like** London?	Yes, he **does**.	No, he **doesn't**.
She **likes** London.	She **doesn't (does not) like** London.	**Does/Doesn't** she **like** London?	Yes, she **does**.	No, she **doesn't**.
It **likes** fish.	It **doesn't (does not) like** fish.	**Does/Doesn't** it **like** fish?	Yes, it **does**.	No, it **doesn't**.
We **like** London.	We **don't (do not) like** London.	**Do/Don't** we **like** London?	Yes, we **do**.	No, we **don't**.
You **like** London.	You **don't (do not) like** London.	**Do/Don't** you **like** London?	Yes, you **do**.	No, you **don't**.
They **like** London.	They **don't (do not) like** London.	**Do/Don't** they **like** London?	Yes, they **do**.	No, they **don't**.

Present continuous

We form the *Present continuous* with **am** / **is** / **are** + the **-ing** form of the verb.

Affirmative	Negative	Questions	Short answers	
I'm (I am) **playing** football.	I'm not (I am not) **playing** football.	**Am** I **playing** football?	Yes, I **am**.	No, **I'm not**.
You're (You are) **playing** football.	You aren't (You're not) **playing** football.	**Are** you **playing** football?	Yes, you **are**.	No, you **aren't**./No, **you're not**.
He's (He is) **playing** football.	He isn't (He's not) **playing** football.	**Is** he **playing** football?	Yes, he **is**.	No, he **isn't**./No, **he's not**.
She's (She is) **playing** football.	She isn't (She's not) **playing** football.	**Is** she **playing** football?	Yes, she **is**.	No, she **isn't**./No, **she's not**.
It's (It is) **raining**.	It isn't (It's not) **raining**.	**Is** it **raining**?	Yes it **is**.	No, it **isn't**./No, **it's not**.
We're (We are) **playing** football.	We aren't (We're not) **playing** football.	**Are** we **playing** football?	Yes, we **are**.	No we **aren't**./No, **we're not**.
You're (You are) **playing** football.	You aren't (You're not) **playing** football.	**Are** you **playing** football?	Yes, you **are**.	No you **aren't**./No, **you're not**.
They're (They are) **playing** football.	They aren't (They're not) **playing** football.	**Are** they **playing** football?	Yes, they **are**.	No, they **aren't**./No, **they're not**.

Present perfect

We form the *Present perfect* with **has** / **have** + the past participle of the verb.

Affirmative	Negative	Questions	Short answers	
I've (I have)	I	**Have** I	Yes, I **have**.	No, I **haven't**.
You've (You have)	You **haven't (have not)**	**Have** you	Yes, you **have**.	No, you **haven't**.
He's (He has)	He	**Has** he	Yes, he **has**.	No, he **hasn't**.
She's (She has) finished.	She **hasn't (has not)** finished.	**Has** she finished?	Yes, she **has**.	No, she **hasn't**.
It's (It has)	It	it	Yes, it **has**.	No, it **hasn't**.
We've (We have)	We	we	Yes, we **have**.	No, we **haven't**.
You've (You have)	You **haven't (have not)**	**Have** you	Yes, you **have**.	No, you **haven't**.
They've (They have)	They	they	Yes, they **have**.	No, they **haven't**.

Present perfect + already / yet

We place **already** between **have / has** and the past participle. **Yet** goes at the end of the sentences.

| I'**ve already** washed the car. | I **haven't done** my homework **yet**. |
| We'**ve already** seen this film. | She **hasn't told** him **yet**. |

Present perfect + ever / never

We place **ever** and **never** between **have / has** and the past participle.

| **Have** you **ever been** to Hollywood? | I'**ve never been** to Hollywood. |
| **Has** she **ever met** a famous person? | She'**s never met** a famous person. |

PAST TENSE

Past simple — was / were

Affirmative	Negative	Questions	Short answers	
I **was** tired.	I **wasn't (was not)** tired.	**Was/Wasn't** I tired?	Yes, I **was**.	No, I **wasn't (was not)**.
You **were** tired.	You **weren't (were not)** tired.	**Were/Weren't** you tired?	Yes, you **were**.	No, you **weren't (were not)**.
He **was** nice.	He **wasn't (was not)** nice.	**Was/Wasn't** he nice?	Yes, he **was**.	No, he **wasn't (was not)**.
She **was** nice.	She **wasn't (was not)** nice.	**Was/Wasn't** she nice?	Yes, she **was**.	No, she **wasn't (was not)**.
It **was** blue.	It **wasn't (was not)** blue.	**Was/Wasn't** it blue?	Yes, it **was**.	No, it **wasn't (was not)**.
We **were** busy.	We **weren't (were not)** busy.	**Were/Weren't** we busy?	Yes, we **were**.	No, we **weren't (were not)**.
You **were** busy.	You **weren't (were not)** busy.	**Were/Weren't** you busy?	Yes, you **were**.	No, you **weren't (were not)**.
They **were** busy.	They **weren't (were not)** busy.	**Were/Weren't** they busy?	Yes, they **were**.	No, they **weren't (were not)**.

Past simple — regular verbs

We add **-ed** to the base form of the verb to form the *Past simple*.

Affirmative	Negative
I lik**ed** London.	I **didn't (did not) like** London.
You laugh**ed** a lot.	You **didn't (did not) laugh** a lot.
He walk**ed** home.	He **didn't (did not) walk** home.
She look**ed** good.	She **didn't (did not) look** good.
It turn**ed** around.	It **didn't (did not) turn** around.
We cook**ed** dinner.	We **didn't (did not) cook** dinner.
You cook**ed** dinner.	You **didn't (did not) cook** dinner.
They lov**ed** the film.	They **didn't (did not) love** the film.

Past time expressions

We use the *Past simple* with these past time expressions.

| then | ago | later | after | one day | finally |

Past simple – irregular verbs

A lot of verbs have an irregular *Past simple*: there are no rules to form this. Here is a list of the most important irregular verbs.

Present	Past simple	Past participle	Present	Past simple	Past participle
be	was/were	been	lay	laid	laid
become	became	become	learn	learnt (learned)	learnt (learned)
begin	began	begun	leave	left	left
blow	blew	blown	let	let	let
break	broke	broken	lie	lay	lain
bring	brought	brought	lose	lost	lost
build	built	built	make	made	made
buy	bought	bought	meet	met	met
catch	caught	caught	put	put	put
choose	chose	chosen	read	read	read
come	came	come	ride	rode	ridden
cut	cut	cut	ring	rang	rung
dig	dug	dug	run	ran	run
do	did	done	say	said	said
draw	drew	drawn	see	saw	seen
dream	dreamt (dreamed)	dreamt (dreamed)	send	sent	sent
drink	drank	drunk	shoot	shot	shot
drive	drove	driven	show	showed	shown (showed)
eat	ate	eaten	sing	sang	sung
fall (asleep)	fell (asleep)	fallen (asleep)	sink	sank (sunk)	sunk
feel	felt	felt	sit	sat	sat
fight	fought	fought	sleep	slept	slept
find	found	found	smell	smelt (smelled)	smelt (smelled)
fly	flew	flown	speak	spoke	spoken
forget	forgot	forgotten	spend	spent	spent
hide	hid	hidden	stand	stood	stood
hurt	hurt	hurt	steal	stole	stolen
get	got	got	swim	swam	swum
get up	got up	got up	take off	took off	taken off
give	gave	given	take	took	taken
go	went	gone	teach	taught	taught
hang	hung	hung	tell	told	told
have	had	had	think	thought	thought
hear	heard	heard	wake (up)	woke (up)	woken (up)
hit	hit	hit	win	won	won
hold	held	held	write	wrote	written
know	knew	known			

FUTURE TENSE

(be) going to

We form the **going to**-future with **am / is / are** + **going to** + the base form of the verb.

Affirmative		Negative	Questions		Short answers
I'm	going to play football.	I'm not	Am I	going to play football?	Yes, I am. / No I'm not.
You're		You aren't (You're not)	Are / Aren't you		Yes, you are. / No, you aren't (you're not).
He's		He isn't (He's not)	Is / Isn't he		Yes, he is. / No, he isn't (he's not).
She's		She isn't (She's not)	Is / Isn't she		Yes, she is. / No, she isn't (she's not).
We're		We aren't (We're not)	Are / Aren't we		Yes, we are. / No, we aren't / we're not.
You're		You aren't (You're not)	Are / Aren't you		Yes, you are. / No, you aren't / you're not.
They're		They aren't (They're not)	Are / Aren't they		Yes, they are. / No, they aren't / they're not.

will-future

We use the **will**-future to talk about future events and to make predictions.

Affirmative	Negative	Questions	Short answers	
I'll (I will) see you tomorrow.	I won't (will not) see you tomorrow.	Will I see you tomorrow?	Yes, I will.	No, I won't (will not).
You'll (You will) see me tomorrow.	You won't (will not) see me tomorrow.	Will you see me tomorrow?	Yes, you will.	No, you won't (will not).
He'll (He will) her tomorrow.	He won't (will not) see her tomorrow.	Will he see her tomorrow?	Yes, he will.	No, he won't (will not).
She'll (She will) see him tomorrow.	She won't (will not) see him tomorrow.	Will she see him tomorrow?	Yes, she will.	No, she won't (will not).
It'll (It will) rain tomorrow.	It won't (will not) rain tomorrow.	Will it rain tomorrow?	Yes, it will.	No, it won't (will not).
We'll (We will) see you tomorrow.	We won't (will not) see you tomorrow.	Will we see you tomorrow?	Yes, we will.	No, we won't (will not).
You'll (You will) see me tomorrow.	You won't (will not) see me tomorrow.	Will you see me tomorrow?	Yes, you will.	No, you won't (will not).
They'll (They will) see you tomorrow.	They won't (will not) see you tomorrow.	Will they see you tomorrow?	Yes, they will.	No, they won't (will not).

Present continuous for future

We use the *Present continuous* to talk about plans and arrangements already made for the future. We often add future time expressions like **tomorrow**, **next weeend**, **next week**.

| What **are you doing** tomorrow? | **I'm going** to a concert in the afternoon. |

SPECIAL VERBS

to be — affirmative, negative

Affirmative	Negative
I'**m** (**I am**) tired.	I'**m not** tired.
You'**re** (**You are**) clever.	You **aren't**/You'**re not** tired.
He'**s** (**He is**) nice.	He **isn't**/He'**s not** nice.
She'**s** (**She is**) in class 3B.	She **isn't**/She'**s not** in class 3B.
It'**s** (**It is**) blue.	It **isn't**/It'**s not** blue.
We'**re** (**We are**) busy.	We **aren't**/We'**re not** busy.
We'**re** (**We are**) busy.	We **aren't**/We'**re not** busy.
They'**re** (**They are**) twelve.	They **aren't**/They'**re not** twelve.

Questions with *be*

Questions	Short answers	
Am I tired?	Yes, you **are**.	No, I'**m not**.
Are/Aren't you tired?	Yes, I **am**.	No, you **aren't**./No, you'**re not**.
Is/Isn't he nice?	Yes, he **is**.	No, he **isn't**./No, he'**s not**.
Is/Isn't she in class 3B?	Yes, she **is**.	No, she **isn't**./No, she'**s not**.
Is/Isn't it blue?	Yes, it **is**.	No, it **isn't**./No, it'**s not**.
Are/Aren't we busy?	Yes, we **are**.	No, we **aren't**./No, we'**re not**.
Are/Aren't you busy?	Yes, you **are**.	No, you **aren't**./No, you'**re not**.
Are/Aren't they twelve?	Yes, they **are**.	No, they **aren't**./No, they'**re not**.

have got / haven't got

The third person singular of **have got** is (*he* / *she* / *it*) **has got**.

Affirmative	Negative	Questions	Short answers	
I'**ve got** (**I have got**) a dog.	I **haven't got** (**have not got**) a dog.	**Have/Haven't** I **got** a dog?	Yes, I **have**.	No, I **haven't**.
You'**ve got** (**You have got**) a dog.	You **haven't got** (**have not got**) a dog.	**Have/Haven't** you **got** a dog?	Yes, you **have**.	No, you **haven't**.
He'**s got** (**He has got**) a dog.	He **hasn't got** (**has not got**) a dog.	**Has/Hasn't** he **got** a dog?	Yes, he **has**.	No, he **hasn't**.
She'**s got** (**She has got**) a dog.	She **hasn't got** (**has not got**) a dog.	**Has/Hasn't** she **got** a dog?	Yes, she **has**.	No, she **hasn't**.
It'**s got** (**It has got**) big ears.	It **hasn't got** (**has not got**) big ears.	**Has/Hasn't** it **got** big ears?	Yes, it **has**.	No, it **hasn't**.
We'**ve got** (**We have got**) a dog.	We **haven't got** (**have not got**) a dog.	**Have/Haven't** we **got** a dog?	Yes, we **have**.	No, we **haven't**.
You'**ve got** (**You have got**) a dog.	You **haven't got** (**have not got**) a dog.	**Have/Haven't** you **got** a dog?	Yes, you **have**.	No, you **haven't**.
They'**ve got** (**They have got**) a dog.	They **haven't got** (**have not got**) a dog.	**Have/Haven't** they **got** a dog?	Yes, they **have**.	No, they **haven't**.

there is / there are

We use **there is** / **there are** to say that something exists in a certain location.

There's a monster in the tree. (= **There is a** monster in the tree.)

There are three frog**s** on the table.

Modal verbs

The main modal verbs are **should / shouldn't**, **have to / don't have to**, **might / might not**, **must / mustn't**, **can / can't**, **could / couldn't**, **will / won't**, **would / wouldn't**, **shall / shall not**, **may / may not**.

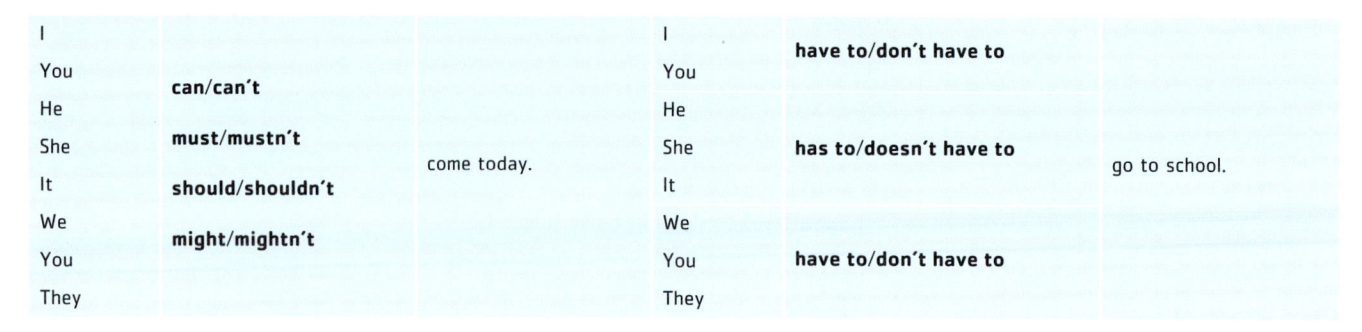

I You He She It We You They	can/can't must/mustn't should/shouldn't might/mightn't	come today.	I You He She It We You They	have to/don't have to has to/doesn't have to have to/don't have to	go to school.

can / can't

Can is a modal verb and is always followed by the base form of a verb. The negative form is **cannot**, often contracted to **can't**.

Affirmative	Negative	Questions	Short answers	
I **can speak** French.	I **can't (cannot) speak** French.	**Can/Can't** I speak French?	Yes, I **can**.	No, I **can't**.
You **can speak** French.	You **can't (cannot) speak** French.	**Can/Can't** you speak French?	Yes, you **can**.	No, you **can't**.
He **can speak** French.	He **can't (cannot) speak** French.	**Can/Can't** he speak French?	Yes, he **can**.	No, he **can't**.
She **can speak** French.	She **can't (cannot) speak** French.	**Can/Can't** she speak French?	Yes, she **can**.	No, she **can't**.
It **can run** fast.	It **can't (cannot) run** fast.	**Can/Can't** it run fast?	Yes, it **can**.	No, it **can't**.
We **can speak** French.	We **can't (cannot) speak** French.	**Can/Can't** we speak French?	Yes, we **can**.	No, we **can't**.
You **can speak** French.	You **can't (cannot) speak** French.	**Can/Can't** you speak French?	Yes, you **can**.	No, you **can't**.
They **can speak** French.	They **can't (cannot) speak** French.	**Can/Can't** they speak French?	Yes, they **can**.	No, they **can't**.

ADVERBS

We generally form adverbs by adding **-ly** to adjectives.

usual – usual**ly**	sad – sad**ly**	furious – furious**ly**

Adverbs of manner

Adverbs of manner show how we do something. Regular adverbs are formed by adding **-ly** to adjectives.

Regular (+ -ly) (regolare)			Irregular (irregolare)	
bad – bad**ly**	quiet – quiet**ly**	happy – happ**ily**	fast – fast	good – well

Adverbs of frequency (always, often, usually, sometimes, never)

0%	→	→	→	100%	We **sometimes** go to the cinema on Fridays.
never	sometimes	often	usually	always	She's **always** happy.

IMPERATIVES

The imperative is equivalent to the base form of the verb (infinitive without **to**). We form the negative imperative with **do not** (**don't**) + the base form of the verb.

Run!	Don't run!
Sit down.	Don't sit down.
Open the window.	Don't open the window.

ARTICLES

Indefinite article

We use the indefinite article **a / an** with countable singular nouns.

a bike	**Before a word beginning with a vowel: a, e, i, o, u**
a teacher	**an** egg /ən ˈeg/
a dog	**an** apple /ən ˈæpl/

Definite article

There is one definite article in English: **the**.

the bike   **the** teacher   **the** dog

NOUNS

Plural nouns – irregular plurals

We add **-s** to singular nouns to make them plural. Nouns ending in consonant + **y** change to **-ies** in the plural. Nouns ending in **f-** or **-fe** change to **-ves** in the plural. Some nouns have an irregular plural.

Regular plurals	dog – dog**s**	snake – snake**s**	cat – cat**s**	baby – bab**ies**	lea**f** – lea**ves**	li**fe** – li**ves**
Irregular plurals	child – children	mouse – mice	foot – feet			

Countable and uncountable nouns

Countable nouns have a singluar and a plural form.   Uncountable nouns only have a singular form.

a chair – two chair**s**   bread   money

PRONOUNS

Question words

Who	**What**	**Where**	**How often**
Who is she?	**What's** your name?	**Where** are you now?	**How often** do you go to the cinema?
Who are you?	**What** eats insects?	**Where** do you live?	
Who likes ice cream?	**What** does your dog eat?		
Who do you like?			

77

this / that, these / those

We use demonstrative adjectives and pronouns to talk about people or things near us (**this** / **these**) or further away (**that** / **those**).

| I like **this** jumper here. | I like **that** jumper over there. | I like **these** shoes here. | I like **those** shoes over there. |

Possessive adjectives

Possessive adjectives always precede the noun.
We do not use an article with possessive adjectives.

I	you	he	she	it	we	they
my	**your**	**his**	**her**	**its**	**our**	**their**

Personal pronouns – subject and object pronouns

We have both subject and object pronouns.
We use **you**, **they** or **one** to talk about people in general.

| Subject | I | You | He | She | It | We | They | Object | me | you | him | her | it | us | them |

one – ones

We use **one** / **ones** to avoid repeating a noun.

What **book** are you reading? **One** about a man travelling around Africa.
What **kind of books** do you like? **Ones** about travel.

some – any

When we don't know the exact quantity of something, we use **some** in positive sentences, **any** in questions and negative sentences. We use **some** in questions when offering or requesting.

some	any	
We've got **some** cheese.	We haven't got **any** cheese.	Is there **any** milk in the fridge?
I've got **some** money.	I haven't got **any** money.	Have we got **any** strawberries?
Would you like **some** soup?	There aren't **any** onions in the kitchen.	Do you want **any** chocolate?

whose + possessive 's

We use **whose** to ask about possession.
We reply by saying the name of the person followed by **'s**.

| **Whose** is this book? | It's Amanda**'s** (book). |
| **Whose** book is this? | It's Harry Potter**'s** (book). |

Possessive pronouns

We use possessive pronouns to show that something belongs to someone.

| It's **my** book. It's **mine**. | It's **his** book. It's **his**. | It's **our** book. It's **ours**. |
| It's **your** book. It's **yours**. | It's **her** book. It's **hers**. | It's **their** book. It's **theirs**. |

PREPOSITIONS

We use prepositions in front of a noun or a pronoun to talk about direction, place or time. (see 'Time prepositions').

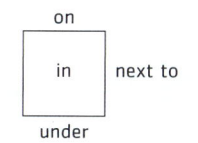

Time prepositions (*in*, *on*, *at*)

My birthday is **on** February 12th / May 28th / September 5th.
My sister's birthday is **in** December / April / June.
The film starts **at** 7 o'clock / half past eight / six forty-five.

We have Maths **in** the morning / in the afternoon.
We go to bed late **at** night.

Prepositions of place (Directions)

| at | by | behind | in | in front of | inside | near |
| next to | on | opposite | outside | over | round | under |

ADJECTIVES

as ... as

We use **as ... as** to say that two persons or things have got the same quality. We use **not as ... as** to say they haven't.

I am **as** intelligent **as** my sister.   Samantha is**n't as** tall **as** Jasmine.

Comparatives & Superlatives

With one syllable adjectives we add **-er** for the comparative and **-est** for the superlative. With adjectives of more than one syllable, we form the comparative with **more** and the superlative with **most**.

My bike is bigg**er** than your bike.   My mum is **the most intelligent** person in our family.

Adjective	Comparative	Superlative	Adjective	Comparative	Superlative
bad	worse	worst	funny	funni**er**	funni**est**
big	bigg**er**	bigg**est**	happy	happi**er**	happi**est**
cold	cold**er**	cold**est**	heavy	heavi**er**	heavi**est**
easy	easi**er**	easi**est**	pretty	pretti**er**	pretti**est**
fast	fast**er**	fast**est**	ugly	ugli**er**	ugli**est**
good	bett**er**	b**est**			
hot	hott**er**	hott**est**	beautiful	**more** beautiful	**most** beautiful
long	long**er**	long**est**	boring	**more** boring	**most** boring
new	new**er**	new**est**	dangerous	**more** dangerous	**most** dangerous

CONJUNCTIONS

Linking words (*and*, *but*, *because*, *so*)

We use linking words (conjunctions) to join main clauses and dependent clauses.

We went to the cinema **and** watched a great film.
　　　　　　　　　　　but it was closed.
　　　　　　　　　　　because we had free tickets.
　　　　　　　　　　　so we missed your call.

So (do/have) I / Neither (do/have) I

If we agree with a positive statement we say **So do I**.
If we agree with a negative statement we say **Neither do I**.
With modal verbs and **have** we repeat the verb, in all other cases we use **do / does / did**.

I **like** rap. – **So do I**.	I **don't like** rock. – **Neither do I**.
I'**ve got** a laptop. – **So have I**.	I **haven't got** a laptop. – **Neither have I**.
I **can** play the piano. – **So can I**.	I **can't play** the piano. – **Neither can I**.
I **went** to the cinema last night. – **So did I**.	I **didn't go** to the cinema last night. – **Neither did I**.

why / because

We use **why** to ask the reason for something. We use **because** in the reply.

Why did you go to the store? – **Because** I needed bread.

QUANTITY / MEASUREMENT

How much is/are...? / How many...?

We use **how much** to ask about quantity or to ask the price of something. We use **how many** to ask about the number of things.

How much ice cream do you eat every day?	**How much** are the trainers?	**How many** pets have you got?	**How many** children are there?

A lot of, not much, not many, a little, a few

a lot of + countable or uncountable nouns.

a lot of money	a lot of biscuits

not much + uncountable nouns, **not many** + countable nouns

not much fun	not many friends

a little + uncountable nouns, **a few** + countable nouns

a little salt	a few hours

Ordinal numbers

Cardinal		Ordinal	Cardinal		Ordinal
1	one	**first**	16	sixteen	sixtee**th**
2	two	**second**	17	seven	seventee**th**
3	three	**third**	18	eighteen	eightee**th**
4	four	four**th**	19	nineteen	nineteen**th**
5	five	fif**th**	20	twenty	twentie**th**
6	six	six**th**	21	twenty-one	twenty-**first**
7	seven	seven**th**	30	thirty	thirtie**th**
8	eight	eigh**th**	40	forty	fortie**th**
9	nine	nin**th**	50	fifty	fiftie**th**
10	ten	ten**th**	60	sixty	sixtie**th**
11	eleven	eleven**th**	70	seventy	seventie**th**
12	twelve	twelf**th**	80	eighty	eightie**th**
13	thirteen	thirteen**th**	90	ninety	nintie**th**
14	fourteen	fourteen**th**	100	hundred	hundred**th**
15	fifteen	fifteen**th**	101	a/one hundred and one	**the (one) hundred and first**